Always ninja

Always love ♡

DONNA LYNN MORANDI

4 F♥CK SAKE

RAISING A PERFECTLY imperfectFAMILY

Table of Contents

Acknowledgments

For my mother, with tremendous gratitude. Without you, I could never be me. To Peter, who has taught me that anything is possible when you believe. And to the Fab4. Thank you for the lessons, the love, and the privilege of being your mother.

Introduction

Securely Insecure about being
Perfectly Imperfect

4 Fuck Sake may seem like a harsh title for a book. And maybe you were a little embarrassed to even buy it, or maybe you were a little intrigued because, dammit, the title spoke to you. For whatever reason, I am sure glad that you bought my book. Now, this book is not meant to be rude or crude, it is meant more of a *"this must be a joke!"* or *"are you kidding me?"* when it comes to parenting. But even those thoughts don't have the same effect that *For Fuck Sake* has. Believe me, I don't go around my house in front of my 4 kids saying, oh, *for fuck sake*, clean up your clothes; *for fuck sake*, I ran out of milk; oh, *for fuck sake*, this bill is due next week. Sounds funny, doesn't it? To be honest, there is a whole lot of chatter going on in my head that never leaves my lips. *For fuck sake* is my go-to chatter phrase. It adds a little humor to whatever is happening at the moment that needs my undivided attention. At best, it lightens the mood. It makes something annoying and inconvenient seem not as serious or intense. Some people count to ten, and some take a deep breath, and even others stomp off mad, too frustrated to deal with it. My reaction is laughter. I laugh at my kids, I laugh at the insanity of raising four very different children and most importantly, I laugh at myself.

I'm not good at a lot of things, but I'll tell you one thing, I'm a pretty good kick ass mother; well, sort of…. I guess it's a matter of perspective. I mean, what makes for a good mother by today's standards? Is it the mother with the straight A student, or the mother with the most athletic kid, or is it the mother that has the most polite or obedient kids? Well if that's the case, then scratch that, I SUCK! My kids aren't perfect, but I know I am a total kick ass mother. They remind me with every hug, every smile, and every secret each one of my kids shares with me. You see, my children run toward me, not away from me, so I know I am doing something right. I view my kids as perfectly imperfect little humans that are learning and growing every single day, and I am okay with that, but again, it depends on your perspective. We all have our own idea of perfection. Some of us feel successful as parents if our kids are happy, healthy, and open-minded, and others feel their success through well-rounded children in both academics and extra-curricular activities, and then there are those of us who are just happy our kids woke up and made it to school on time. I am sure most parents would feel pretty successful at parenting if they had a kid that had strong attributes in academics, athletics, and school in general, since it takes up a big part of their day. But let's face it, no one is perfect; not us, not our kids, and not our spouses; and for the most part we realize that the hard part is admitting that even moms can be insecure about our imperfections. The thing is, we know our kids are counting on us.

Announcement: It is human nature to have insecurities, and to be perfectly imperfect. In the pages ahead, I hope you can laugh and cry and relate to me through my imperfect journey of motherhood, as I face my fears and failures. I am sure you will be able to identify with many of the stories that I share with you. And through it all, I hope that you can embrace your own perfectly imperfect family. And be proud of who you are and what you do.

Chapter 1

Well… This Wasn't the Plan

IN MANY WAYS, I LIVE A LIFE STRAIGHT RIGHT OUT OF THE 1950s; not that there is anything wrong with that. It's just that I am aware of it. I just never intended my life to turn out like this, but here I am: a suburban housewife. I went to college and had dreams and aspirations of a career with power and money; and yet here I am making baked apple slices while doing the laundry, straightening up the living room, and thinking about what's for dinner. In about an hour the chaos will be arriving. The Fab Four will be getting home from school. From there it will be pick-up time, drop-off time, sports time, homework time, dinner time, bath time, and the well- anticipated bedtime. I am sure many mothers have different routines than me that they find to be interesting and exciting to them. But every day welcoming home the Fab Four after their time away at school is what keeps my soul thriving.

I sometimes wonder where I would be had I not gotten married and had children. Would I have an apartment in the city? Dress in name brand clothing? Eat out at fancy restaurants? Have sophisticated discussions with important people? Most importantly, would I be happy? Let me say this, I am at peace with where my life has led me and the choices I have made, but it certainly wasn't the plan. I can't remember a specific time when I made the decision that my life would be focused on family, but I know it was a deliberate decision.

I think my interest in having a big family started when I moved to Levittown, New York. So many other families with kids were moving there as well. I have always loved all the hustle and bustle of a big family. The different personalities, the energy, the love, and the laughter. There's a certain pride in having 4 kids. It's like telling the world, we are bad ass. In fact, if I can turn back time I would have more children. Again, that was never the plan. I was motivated and prepared to live a life of adventure and in many ways, I do live that life, but just not as I originally conjured in my mind. Like many young girls, I had my sights set high on "taking over the world." With age and wisdom, I have come to realize that my intentions did become a reality, except "my world" became much more intimate.

I have no problem leaving my house with my hair wrapped casually into pigtails bouncing in the air, no make-up on my face, and wearing my Target-brand sun dress and cheap flip-flops in my small suburban town called Levittown. I look around and everywhere there are moms in expensive heels, moms with flawless makeup, moms with places to go and people to see, and I can't help feeling so out of my element. It's not lost on me that living in Levittown is nothing short of ironic. If you Google "Levittown" you will learn that it was the first suburb in America, designed to provide affordable housing. It became the symbol of the "American Dream" after World War II. Levittown, for all intents and purposes, was built on conformity. The homes all looked the same, the yards all looked the same, and the people all looked the same. So how did a person like me end up in a place like this? Good question.

To say I was sheltered growing up in the small town of Bayville, on the North Shore of Long Island, New York, would be an understatement. As a child, I played with my Cabbage Patch dolls and enjoyed the regular girl things. As I got older I became more of a tomboy and loved playing outside with the neighborhood kids. We would spend hours playing ring and run, running bases, soccer, and monkey in the middle. It was a great neighborhood filled with family barbecues. We all had a sense of safety. But even then, my plan was never to be some great stay-at-home mom. I was always looking forward to leaving my small town and venturing off into the great big world.

When I was 14, my grandmother took me to her native country of England. I fell in love with the culture and independence of traveling to another country. That first overseas trip got me hooked on life outside of my small town.

I worked three jobs my senior year of high school and saved up all my money so that I could return to Europe, this time with my cousin Christina. We traveled to England and France. Christina was older than me and already very cultured and educated. Traveling with her made my experience even more rich and rewarding. Being with her changed the way I viewed myself, the world, and how I wanted to live my life. I began to view the world as something I wanted to participate in, and experience on a deeper level, more than I had in the past. In many ways she helped transform this small-minded Long Island girl to someone who dreams bigger and greater.

Entering college, I was focused on making a name for myself. I was driven and felt proud that I was a student at Roger Williams University, in Bristol, Rhode Island. Growing up feeling stupid or less than, I never felt like I had the ability to succeed in college. Between my mother's true belief in me, Christina's influence, and my own determination, I knew that I had to go to college. I decided to enroll in the paralegal program and did well in all my classes. I was outspoken, confident, and probably a bit obnoxious. I was able to party at school and still maintain my focus on my future. At a young age, I had the confidence to know that anything I put my mind to would become my reality. I credit that to my reading disability and my mother's belief that hard work pays off. And it did. I graduated from college feeling proud and hopeful about my future. Somewhere along the way, however, my focus changed because I fell in love.

Although I didn't realize it at the time, college prepared me so much for motherhood. Many people go to college expecting to earn an education, to advance in their careers, and to learn life academically and socially. Although that may be true, I have learned so much more about life and being a mother by attending college. There, I formed friendships and bonds with people that I am still close with today. Just recently, I met up with a few of my college girlfriends at Roger Williams University for our 20th year reunion. We spent the weekend exploring the campus, reminiscing, and hanging out at the local bars where once we were frequent customers. Our lives have changed, and so has the campus, but the bond created from our years in college is still very much intact. We experienced our transition into adulthood together.

We cried. We laughed. We talked about serious stuff, and many times we were downright hysterical! Oh, how I loved college life!

One incident in particular stands out. It was the weekend before Halloween and there were many parties going on off campus. My friend, Randy, invited both me and our friend, Joel, to a Halloween party. Assuming it was a costume party, Joel and I went out to find the perfect costume for the event. After searching through thrift stores on our very limited college budget, we decided that I would go as a clown and he would be Superman (cape and all). The thought of going to a Halloween costume party where we knew virtually no one was quite appealing to both Joel and me. We arrived fashionably late and already a little buzzed from cheap beer and no- name cigarettes. Imagine our surprise when we realized that we were the only two dressed in complete Halloween costumes. While we were pretty shocked ourselves, we looked at each other, shrugged our shoulders and said, "We're in!" We canvassed the party like we owned the place. The stares and whispers didn't bother us much, probably because we were half in the bag, but more so because we were the most popular people there and we knew it. Who *wouldn't* want to hang out with the clown and her Superman? Once we made the rounds and everyone got to know us, we initiated a college drinking card game called Asshole. Now if you don't know what that is you can Google it. You will also find the "official rules." I'm not kidding. Before long, Joel and I had total command of the entire game and party. Almost immediately, Joel was the president and I was his vice president, both positions are of the highest ranking in the game of Asshole and we took our jobs seriously. In college having that title at a party was golden, and usually short-lived. Taking full advantage of our status, we became increasingly obnoxious, forcing those "under" our ranking to drink. We knew we took the game too far when we shouted, "If you are not wearing a costume, drink!" and everyone started groaning, which ipitated the end of the game. Joel and I decided to mingle among e of the other guests, while exploring the house. We soon found ourselves in master bedroom, and within minutes we were passed out on the bed. And then... I threw up. It was on the sheets, the pillows, the bedspread, there was even some that splashed on to a stuffed cat that was strategically placed between the throw pillows. That's when we knew that it was time to go. Stumbling, yet feeling like we were in stealth mode, we slipped out of the back door, unnoticed. I remember that two-mile walk back to campus. We laughed so hard we couldn't contain ourselves. It was an absurd night to begin with when, as strangers, we arrived at a Halloween party as Superman and his sidekick, the clown. To this day, it is one of the funniest stories I've ever been part of, and one of the many times that I felt like *for fuck sake*, here I am in a full clown costume: me, the rock star, accompanied by my Superman Joel.

The lesson I learned that night was no matter what, keep your head held high, and even if it's in only in your own mind, know that you're a rock star, and walk around believing it. College was fun and I made the greatest friends. Roger Williams University is also where I met my future husband.

To this day, I will never truly understand how the nicest, smartest, and most giving man I have ever known selected me to spend the rest of his life with. Our first date was a set up by my very dear friend, Meg. She knew both of us and lied about each other's interest in the other. I know, not too romantic, but that's how our story began. A set up by one of my best friends. Peter and I were in a real estate law class together. He was there for the real estate, and I was there for the law part. Meg thought that we would make a perfect pair, so she used her charm to get us together. She asked me what I thought of that guy, Peter and I responded, "He's okay. He's smart and seems nice." She asked Peter the same of me and he responded, "She's kind of cute."

Neither of us knew that she was sharing the information with the other. She told me that Peter was crazy about me and couldn't keep his eyes off of me and she told Peter the same thing about me. In other words, she lied to perform a love connection. The real story is more like I was a struggling student (probably because I was partying too much), and I thought, *wow!* this guy is really smart. Maybe he'll help me out in this class. And he thought I was fun and a free spirit. He found me intriguing and that kept his interest. My college friends thought we were an unlikely pair and we'd never make it as a couple. Their reason? I was the party girl and he was the guy who graduated # 5 in our class. What they didn't realize was that Peter and I had the same core values, the same sense for adventure, and the same respect and loyalty to family. Peter had something that I never found with anyone before. He was decisive. He knew what he wanted. He was focused on his future, he was ambitious, and he was kind. One of the first things he said to me when we began dating was, "Buckle up, if you stick with me, you're in for the ride of your life." And he was right. Now, over 20 years later, that has been absolutely true. Peter has accomplished more than I think either of us ever dreamed. He's a good father, a good husband, a wonderful provider, and a great friend. A testament of his love for me is that he often says, "In the 20-plus years I've known you, you haven't changed a bit. You're still zany, fun and unpredictable!" I'm not quite as fun and carefree as I was when I was younger, but all things considered I am still free at heart and find happiness in waking up every single day.

After college, I was offered two jobs in Boston. As a child I always dreamed of living there, so I figured that was a good sign. I visited Boston with my family and loved the New England charm. Peter and I started a life together in Massachusetts. At a young age, we were both ambitious and building names and careers for ourselves. At the time, I was working for a computer software company in the contract negotiating department. I loved the work and the money was great. My only problem was that I didn't like Boston like I thought I would. It was way too cold, and I was used to the outspoken, up-front New York lifestyle. One cold and rainy afternoon, I started packing my suitcase. When Peter came home, he asked, "Are you going to visit your folks down in New York?" I replied with much calm: "Nope. I'm moving back to New York. Then I added, "Are you coming?" Without hesitation, Peter said yes.

We moved to New York with no jobs, no connections, and yet somehow, we made it work. We didn't have a lot of money, but we were young and had a lot of love. In your early 20s you truly don't need a lot. We got married at 23, and everyone around us thought we were too young and crazy to make such a commitment. To add to our spontaneity, we immediately bought a house. We landed in Levittown by accident, basically because it was (at the time) affordable and close to the train station. At the time, Levittown was "providing families the domestic component of the American dream," or so it was advertised that way when it was first built.

I had no idea what owning a house entailed, and had no business doing it, but took the risk of homeownership, never imagining that we would actually grow roots. My father used to refer to my house as a "Shabanga." He used that word endearingly, to say that we got a great deal on a real shithole, but shabanga just sounded better. From the wood panels inside the den, to the linoleum floors in the kitchen, to the bathroom where you had to duck to enter, the place was a wreck.

At the closing of our first home we had a total of $84 in the bank. We lived on the dollar menu items from McDonald's, which we had to split and were able to survive because we had each other and a very good sense of humor. I remember one day my mother came over to my half-renovated home and said, "If your marriage survives this, it will survive anything." Now, twenty years later, I am happy to say, so far so good. We have had many ups and downs, but by the grace of God we are still here. Through the years, I have learned many lessons about life and marriage. The biggest lesson learned is to always have a good sense of humor because this shit is just plain Cray Cray.

Chapter 2

And So, It Begins...

IN 2001, AFTER THE SEPTEMBER 11ᵀᴴ TERRORIST ATTACK, I found it to be a very strange time in my life, in my marriage, and in this country. My father had been battling cancer, my husband was working crazy hours to build a career and a name for himself, the country was in despair, and I felt completely alone. I would come home from a job I didn't like, in the house I didn't want, and sit alone at my kitchen table and eat my dinner in deafening silence. I knew that this loneliness and unhappiness was leading me down the road to depression. I felt a constant tug that something was missing from my life. I had no idea what it was or even why I felt that way. At the time, I wasn't necessarily ready to have children, but I was certainly excited at the thought and possibility that it was in my distant future.

When I talked with Peter about having a baby, he was less than enthusiastic, but would do anything for me. After about three months of trying, we decided to make a doctor's appointment. We received devastating news that I would not be able to bear my own children. My father was dying, I was lonely, I felt like I had no purpose, and then to find out I could not get pregnant gave me an overwhelming sense of sadness. I spent many nights crying alone, feeling like a failure, and angry because everywhere I looked, women were pregnant or having kids left and right, and I wasn't. It reminded me of when I was in school, and all the other kids were reading and excelling, and there I was floundering and failing, again. It was a devastating and a sad time for me that brought back many insecurities from my childhood. Before I received the news from my doctor, I had already started stocking up on pregnancy tests because it never entered my mind that I would not be able to bear children. Regardless of what my doctor said, every month I would still check.

Then finally, out of sheer disgust and anger, and in defiance of my expected reality, I opened my last pregnancy test box and reached for the strip to pee on. This act of me sitting on the toilet with tears streaming down my face was anything but familiar, because my blurred eyes saw that positive sign. How could that be? As much as I wanted to see that, I was shocked when I did. I was afraid to get my hopes up, but with my heart beating out of my chest, I rushed to the drugstore to buy three more boxes of pregnancy tests.

I remember spending the night drinking a ridiculous amount of water and urinating on one strip after another. They were all positive. Positive. Positive. Positive. I was going to be a mother! I spent no time getting to my doctor to verify the tests, and as it turned out, the reason why my hormone levels were so off kilter was because I was already pregnant! Don't ask. I have no idea why they didn't know that before. Now I was crying tears of joy, tears of hope, and tears of - *for fuck sake, I'm going to have a baby!*

Something magical happened. From that moment on, I no longer felt alone. I dreamed about the future and knew that this child would forever change my life. Once William was born, I knew my calling. I knew that no amount of money or career advancements would ever give me the self-fulfillment that this little child gave me. I quit my job, walked away from my career, and left behind the person who I was before my precious son was born.

It was not always financially easy, and it was not always a bed of roses, but I just knew that this was my path, my journey in the life that I knew I wanted to lead. Being a stay-at-home mom is not glamorous. You do not get the accolades that you do at a job, you do not get a pay-check, and sometimes you do not even get a shower. But for me, I got something that money couldn't buy; something that would last a lifetime. I got to never feel lonely again, and there is no price tag for that.

As a child and into adulthood, I would find myself surrounded by so many people who loved me and cared for me, but for some reason I still felt lonely. I had no idea that deep loneliness could disappear by having children. In my heart and in my head, I finally felt fulfilled. Being older now, I understand that it really had nothing to do with having children as much as it had to do with finding myself, being comfortable within my heart, and being confident that I am who I am and happy to be this person.

When I was pregnant, I didn't think much about breastfeeding. I was young and just happy to be having a baby. Once William was born and the nurse put him in my arms she immediately put him directly to my breast. I was having a little trouble getting him to latch on, and a wonderful lactation consultant named Christine, happened to be on duty. She was passionate about breast-feeding and helped me learn how to do it correctly. Her kindness and patience changed my life and opened my mind and heart to breast-feeding. Once I got the hang of it, I loved it. I breast-fed all four of my children each for over a year. I loved the feeling of nourishing their tiny little bodies, I enjoyed the closeness of our skin together, and I cherished the time that I got to spend with each baby while nursing. I was told that when you breast-feed, your children grow to be smarter, you bond better with them, and they are less likely to get sick. For me, most of that is true.

Let me tell you what my experience hasn't been. Now don't get me wrong, I absolutely loved breast-feeding. It was probably one of my most favorite things about having a baby. I'm sure that there is some science behind all the benefits of breastfeeding - that children may be brighter, more alert, and healthier. However, my children get sick just as much as any other child, if not more. In my home every season, we have had everything from the common cold to numerous cases of bron-chitis, strep throat, and pneumonia. My children catch just about every germ known to mankind. And while we are on the subject about the benefits of breastfeeding, I will begin by saying that I love my kids, but there is no Albert Einstein in the bunch. They are great, fun kids, but geniuses? Not so much. When all is said and done, at the end of the day, I am left with droopy boobs, sick kids, and average students. Although I loved and cherish my breastfeeding experience, *for fuck sake*, I was bamboozled into thinking I was going to have germ-fighting geniuses. Not the case.

I will admit. I was one of those mothers I came to avoid as I matured into motherhood. My first two children were two years apart and they were perfect. Perfectly dressed, perfectly behaved, and I was perfectly happy. They would hold my hand, cooperate on commands, get along well with each other, and overall, made my days pretty easy. (I know, I know, insert eye roll, but keep reading to make yourself feel better.) I used to watch other mothers with screaming kids, running and jumping all over the place and I would think, wow that looks rough! How naïve of me. Little did I realize then that my time was coming. Two and a half years after Emma was born, I gave birth to Benjamin. From the time of conception, I knew this child was going to be my wildcard.

It started when I was told that he was not going to make it, and that eventually the pregnancy would terminate. I had a tear in my uterus and there was a big chance he would drown in my blood, which would result in a miscarriage. I was encouraged to end the pregnancy. This was a hard decision, and one that I would not make. Having suffered from an earlier failed pregnancy, there was no way in my heart and mind that I would ever be able to voluntarily terminate my pregnancy. In all reality, I had a strong intuition that my son would be healthy. And boy was I right. I went against the advice of my doctor and left this in God's hands.

Benjamin was born 10 days early and almost in the front seat of my Honda Odyssey. Seventeen minutes after I arrived at the hospital, I was holding my healthy baby boy. No drugs, no epidural, no pain medicine, no time to even think. He was coming into this world quickly and frantically and has been the same way ever since. As a toddler, Benjamin was more of a hot-tempered kid, but still, even with his rambunctiousness, I had things under control. I was feeling pretty satisfied with my adjustment to this high-spirited child. Motherhood was back to being easy. Then. I. Had. Matthew. He was my wake-up call. At times, he did me in. Always a spectacle everywhere we went, whether it be crying or running amok, this child was a handful. He was getting his money's worth for entering this world. He would take the poop out of his diaper and smear it all over the walls. That was new. Somehow, I was able to avoid cleaning poop off my walls for my first three children. It just never came up; or in this case, out of the diaper. I have a pretty good sense of humor and I actually laughed at it the first time, chuckled the second time, and even smirked the third time. But by the fourth time, I looked at him squarely in his eyes and asked, "Seriously kid, what is it with you and poop?"

Matthew was my one kid that got into everything, from climbing counters, to climbing into the refrigerator, to drinking milk from the carton. There were no limits to his curiosity! One time when he was just three, he walked out of the house, unnoticed by everyone, and a neighbor down the block brought him home. He was THAT child. I quickly knew that for the sanity of our family and the rest of society, he needed to be the last child. I also knew deep in my heart that he was meant to be my last child. It was a feeling of completion. Like everyone was here now. My four children had arrived and now my family was complete.

The kids are getting older now, and life at home consists of noisy… well, noisy everything. Some days I perch on a chair at the counter in the kitchen and wait for the Fab Four to filter home from school. I'm in the background keeping an eye on things in case they need something. As the boys file in, they know I will come up with whatever they ask for. I always give them space to unwind from their day at school. I'm around, but I am quiet. Last home is usually Emma. She is generally running late because of her after-school activities, and will frantically run past me, announcing, "Don't ask!" and I'm okay with that. She knows I'm here for her, but she also knows I won't push her to talk.

Each of my kids knows that I'm the "go – to" when they need me. But honestly, in most cases, they have each other. As the boys arrive home, the volume goes up and they're all over the kitchen looking for a snack. I don't mind the tornado that just got here; I've been waiting for them all day. There are times when I hear their giggling and nervous *shhhh* sounds. And every now and then I will look up, nod my head, and smile. I know that whatever mess is going on, they are making memories that they will talk about years from now. More importantly, they are building a bond with their siblings and learning skills that can only be taught through experience. From snow forts, to homemade water slides, to failed pranks, to hopping fences, to sibling secrets... this is what makes childhood special. I know this because the imagination my kids have is incredible. I'm not just saying that. One time we drove up to Connecticut to watch my husband complete his first half Ironman competition. It was early in the morning and there were many hours of sitting and literally doing nothing in between each event. So, my kids decided to play baseball. One of them found a rock and when they went to bat, each used one of their flip-flop to swing at the rock. Baseball with a flip-flop and a rock. Ingenious! That's what my kids do. They find the fun in everything. They say absurd things and make up crazy stories and use their imaginations in ways I never thought of when I was their age. They play together and work together and genuinely hold that bond together. They aren't mean; in fact, they are kind human beings.

In raising my children, I created an environment that allows them to be kids. One period of time in my life that brings me joy to remember was when my children were two, four, six, and eight. I loved saying that when people would ask how old they were. I would always reply, "2-4-6-8," and without hesitation, the kids would chant, "Who do we appreciate? Mommy!" They adored me! These little children of mine absolutely adored me! Their smiles were from the simplest of things. An extra scoop of mac & cheese, a lollipop after lunch, a favorite show on TV, and milk and homemade cookies. I loved that time when they were young, because they felt safe, they were happy, there was no stress in their lives, and they only knew happiness and love. It was a joyous time for me, such a special season. Now when I look back at pictures of them at that age, I remember it with such joy.

Yes, it was chaotic, but it was pure, it was real, and it was fun. As my kids have grown, they adore me in other ways. My teenagers like to antagonize me, roll their eyes at me, and make fun of me for what I'm wearing, or what I say, or how I dance, or how I look. Beneath all of that making fun, there is love. It's teenage love, yes; but it is love. My eight and 10-year-old follow suit with their older siblings, but when the older ones are not looking, the younger ones cuddle up next to me, hold me tight, tell me they love me, and still have the sweet innocence of youth. Actually, my older kids do the same thing when no one is around. Having private time has allowed me to bond separately and uniquely with each of my children, which in turn has strengthened all our relationships.

As I sit on the front porch in my white rocking chair that my mother gave to me as a gift long ago, I could hear the commotion going on in the backyard and pandemonium ensuing inside. I can't get myself to get off the rocking chair to deal with it. I need a moment, a moment of peace, a moment of calmness, a moment that I can gather my thoughts and then go back in and figure out what the hell is going on. I figured that some Nerf gun game got out of hand or an argument over the last ice cream cone got out of control, or perhaps one kid was breathing too heavy on another kid. Who knows with this parenting thing? In fact, you never quite know what your days are going to bring. It's part of the wonderment, it's part of the stress, and it's all the parts that I both cherish and detest.

My rocking chair outside my front door represents so much to me. It represents a gift from my mom. Often, when I am rocking, I wonder where she used to go to catch her breath. She always seemed so in control and happy. I never quite knew if she ever felt like me, or if she was genuinely unfazed by the stresses of motherhood. If she was overwhelmed I rarely knew it, and that was both a gift and a curse. She was patient and kind. Those moments when I freak out on my kids, it makes me feel like a failure. And then I wonder, do our kids recognize it when we are stressed out? Are we as good at hiding it as we think? Or are we just as transparent as we hope we're not?

The rocking chair also represents a time when I can watch the world out front. I watch my children play outside, I listen to them play from a distance. I see the cars passing by and other busy parents rushing their kids to and from all sorts of activities. In the summertime, the rocking chair means so much to me because that's where I go in the late, late night when the kids are in bed and I am winding down from the day. I sit and read or just watch the lightning bugs or listen to the crickets. So many important thoughts and life-changing decisions have come from my time rocking in that chair. What I really mean to say is, the rocking chair that my mother bought me represents a small, sacred place in this home that is mine. It is where I sit to think and debate with myself over all sorts of things. I think it's important to have a place. It doesn't have to be a rocking chair, it could be anywhere you go to catch your breath, rethink, and rejuvenate. Sometimes, as I'm sitting in the rocking chair, I conjure memories of when my kids were little, and life seemed much simpler. They would play in the driveway, making towns out of chalk, ride their bikes, skateboards, and roller blades. They would play Toss on the grass, and I would sit there, watching intently, wondering where their imaginations would take them next.

Although I miss those days and long for that peacefulness and simplicity, I appreciate the fact that they are growing, they are coming into their own, and they are thriving. Don't get me wrong, there was a time when having four children and a husband who was starting his career and was barely ever home, led to some hectic times, but they were also safe times. I knew where my kids were, I knew who they were with, I knew what they were eating, what they were watching, and what they were wearing. Those were challenging times, but I had control over everything. It was all about me showing them how to live and them, with very little resistance, abiding by what I said. We would choose between a museum or the park, peanut butter and jelly, or crackers and cheese. Simple little decisions were made throughout the day, and together those conversations and decisions formed who they were going to be and who I was going to be as a parent. Now, as we have two teenagers and two children slowly making their way to become teenagers, I don't have that same control. I don't get to decide who their friends are, what they play, and who they spend time with. I don't get to choose what they wear and what they think because now they are their own people. Truth is, I don't have the same effect on them as I used to. Oh, *for fuck sake,* there was even a time when their Dad or I were the only two in charge of the TV remote! Giving up control is a hard thing to do, but my kids have taught me that it was a necessary one. I always try to teach them by example. They know my values include being a good, kind, and confident person. Their respect and love for me aside, they are each becoming their own person. I cannot force them to be as friendly as I am or to exercise as much as I do. They are who they are and I respect and love each one of them for that. Each day, as I watch them stretch and grow, the separation between mother and child becomes more and more apparent. So far, I am pleased with what I am seeing. As they get older and develop into their own people, I admire their confidence. I sit on my rocking chair even now and swell with pride as I think about the people they are becoming and how those little decisions in their toddler years were making them who they are now. Having opportunities to make little decisions at a very young age helped them to make good decisions now. They are not anxious, indecisive, or angry people. They are level-headed and happy.

I sometimes dream about going back to the time when they were just babies and reliving it just for a day, just for a moment. Oh, to capture those days again! To see the innocence in their eyes and the trust in their heart. They truly believed that anything I said or did was amazing. My Fab Four made me feel like a million bucks. They do so today as well, but they are older now and it takes far more effort to make them outwardly admire or care about me. With my two oldest, I find that they show it in their own secret teenage ways: a smile, a flower, a hug, and sometimes a little note from my daughter.

If you are like me, you wonder what impact you are truly having on your children. Did you spend enough time? Did you do enough and say enough? I wonder, do they know right from wrong? Do they know their limits when it comes to Mom and Dad? I hope the answer is yes. When I deliver my message in the most respectful and articulate way, my expectations are clear, so there is no room for debate or amnesia.

When they do fall below what I expect of them, I'm not shy to tell them, so they understand where I'm coming from. That's really all I need to do, and then I hope that they correct their behavior. I also know that they will learn a thing or two along the way. My rocking chair has provided me with a safe haven to think, to be present, and to reflect and smile about the way it used to be. While rocking, I feel and express those emotions that my children will never see. They are private and I cherish them. I will always cling to my memories when I am in my rocking chair. It is so much more than a spot to sit and watch my kids grow. It is the chair that I sat in as I worked through my thoughts and ideas about everything that was best for my kids. This wonderful gift from my mother has worn through the years, but the memories will always be fresh.

Chapter 3

Meet The Fab Four: William, Emma, Benjamin, and Matthew

I'VE BEEN CALLING MY CHILDREN THE FAB FOUR SINCE Matthew was born. In fact, they are known around town and by family and friends as the Fab Four. I love the name. I love what it represents, and I love how they uphold that title. Having four children in seven years was probably the best thing I could've done in building my family. In fact, if I could turn back time I would have had more children and even closer in age. For the most part, I love how my family interacts with one another. I love all the giggles and laughter and practical jokes. I love all the mischief and fun that goes on in our home. I raised them to be good friends. I always insist that they treat each other kindly and that in our home we speak lovingly and with respect. I insist on this because when my children are out in the world, I cannot control how they are treated, but in my home, I can, and I will.

I have learned that when you enforce specific behaviors every day, and you are consistent in giving your kids feedback on how they are doing, they will embrace the friendship with their siblings and the bond with their family. I know it sounds hard to believe, but it is true. My kids enjoy the company of each other, and they enjoy their positions in our family. It works for all of us. They make up games and stories and activities and just play together. At any given moment I may hear a crash, followed by a thump, and led by a piercing scream that eventually turns into laughter and giggles. Today, however, there's not enough of that. Everyone is in such a rush to get to organized sports and after school activities, and rushing here and there, then back to here has just about taken over our lives. *Oh, for fuck sake,* if you know what I mean.

I know that having 4 kids was the right decision for my family. I've always been someone with great instincts. Good gut feelings, good intuition, good vibe – whatever you want to call it. I always knew in my gut what to do. From a very young age, I was able to understand things and make decisions accordingly, based on what I felt inside. From allowing my kids to experience life differently than others, to working on a strong relationship with each of my children, I don't spend much time second guessing myself. Now that I'm older and wiser and more mature, even things that might seem irrational or don't make sense to others, if I get a gut feeling about it, I know to trust it. Whether it has to do with finances, relationships, or other major decisions, I trust my instincts and I do not sway once I make a decision. To be able to use my instincts in such a positive way is a gift; one that I am thankful for.

When we are younger and more insecure, we are never quite convinced that we are making the right decision, but the older you get, the more you gain a certain sense of stability when it comes to your own intuition. I see with my own children, how they waiver with decisions. Many times, they will be so uncertain that they can change their mind a number of times before making a final decision. One of the greatest benefits of growing older is that you trust yourself more than you trust others, you feel more comfortable in your own skin and in situations that may be uncomfortable, and you have a better understanding of what's important and what's just noise. I feel this way about parenting as well. I let things slide that to me are "just noise." I often give my children more freedom than most because bedtimes and other common rules, for me, are just "noise." However, for all my "anti-noise theories," I do expect that when I ask them to do a simple task like put away their shoes, or clean their room, or maybe straighten up their closet, they don't give me such a hard time. It's one of those moments where I want to say, oh, *for fuck sake*, just do it! Just do it!

I am sure many parents feel the same way; we all have those buttons that our kids can find to press. At times, it may feel like they just keep taking and we keep giving. Then suddenly after all the giving we do and all the taking they take, we blow a fuse and have to reset the rules. Just about that time my kids look at me like I am completely out of my mind, and I am just a crazy lady screaming over a small infraction like a piece of lint on the carpet. What they are missing is the bigger picture. It's not the lint on the carpet, or their shoes not lined up straight in the closet that makes me go crazy. Actually, none of it has anything to do with my outburst. Remember how I mentioned all the small stuff building into the bigger picture? That is the exact point. It's about the small minor infractions that occur over and over again, while everything else is building up. It's the moment when you want to scream at the top of your lungs from deep within your soul and say, *for fuck sake,* line up the shoes and pick up the lint and don't ask any more questions!

Each one of my children has a uniquely different personality. William is kind, creative, and witty. Emma is organized, artsy, focused, and caring. Benjamin is my sports kid: he's active, health-conscious, and incredibly sarcastic. Matthew, my last child who holds that title with a badge of honor, is a little bit of the first three, but with the earned sassiness of being the last child. He's used to being spoiled and getting his way, but he's turning into a kind, curious, and loving boy. All four of my kids are a little piece of me, a little piece of their father, and a whole lot of their own individuality. They all have a special relationship with each other. They get along and each has a favorite sibling, which may change from time to time, day to day, hour to hour, and sometimes minute to minute. It's just part of having siblings. William is usually the first to make up some kind of crazy game and the others will follow blindly, not really caring about the trouble that they're about to get into. On one memorable occasion, Matthew came running into the kitchen grabbing a bunch of cleaning supplies and went darting out the door screaming, "Mom, it's better if you just don't ask!" As a mother, I have learned from my kids that sometimes it is best not to ask. I can almost guarantee that there will be a mess and something will probably be broken, but – and this is the big but – the memories and relationships that they are building together means more than the mess or whatever might be broken. I think that's why my kids are so close with each other. I don't get involved in their arguments. I let them work it out. Far too many parents try to referee everything. I believe my children need to navigate their relationships with each other and develop their position in our family as being one of four children. I give them the freedom to be kids. I give them the freedom to be siblings. I give them the freedom to be each other's friend and be each other's family. It's not without fights or frustrations, there's plenty of that; but for the most part, there's love, there's laughter, and there's a lot of chaos. And frankly, I wouldn't want it any other way.

Mothers and Daughters.

There is a torrential downpour happening outside right now, and my 13-year-old daughter exclaims, "Mom, we have to go shopping, right now!" It's Tuesday evening and my little beauty decides she must get to a store to buy some acrylic paint for a project she's working on. I oblige and head out into the crazy weather, drive the mile to the store, and we shop. While there, I find some great sales that I just couldn't say no to, then I remember that I have this fantastic coupon for Kohl's and decide we must go there as well. Our drenched bodies walk into Kohls, splashing through the aisle, as we are giggling uncontrollably at how ridiculous we both must look, then start shopping for things we don't particularly need or want, but because we have a coupon we must have them. For me, that's the great thing about having a daughter, she's always up to shop, to chat, and to enjoy a stop at Starbucks. I absolutely adore my daughter. In fact, everyone knows it. Her friends, her friend's parents, the community, my family; I just love this kid.

Emma is so much more like her father than me and I find her incredibly interesting. In fact, I'm fascinated by her. I love that I have a friend to talk to when I'm sad, because she cares in a way that my boys could never do. She's compassionate and kind and thoughtful and loving and I look at her in awe, that this child is my daughter. Now, I know many people have theories about teenage daughters and mothers, I get that, and I'm ready for it. But my relationship with my daughter is pretty strong. She trusts me and I trust her. She is ambitious like her father, and witty like me. Having a daughter and having someone I know I can rely on for all the wonderful mother-daughter moments is such a blessing and I'm grateful that I get to experience it. From bows in her hair, to getting her ears pierced, to designer clothes, to watching her play sports and music, to taking her to concerts and waiting three hours on line just to meet a YouTuber, as well as her eye rolling and long ass stories about things I have no idea what she's talking about most of the time, I truly enjoy it all. I am proud and honored to be her mother. And while other mothers may complain about all the *fucks sakes* that their teenage daughters bring, (including myself), I still wouldn't trade it for the world.

And about those boys.

I got three of them. They are dirty, have fart contests, find the most disgusting things interesting, and are constantly running, jumping, or tackling one another. But they are my boys. My three boys. There's something special about each one. I love how kind William is, I love how sporty Benjamin is, and I love how inventive Matthew is. They each have their strengths and to watch them together is magic. Their "play" is nothing short of a disaster. It's their wonderful, brotherly disaster. And I embrace it all. The mud, the grossness, the climbing and jumping off of things they shouldn't be, the dares, and the nonstop eating. Honestly, they fascinate me. Maybe because I only had one brother and was never really around a lot of boys. Frankly, my brother wasn't a typical boy that did all the nonstop gross things that you might expect.

The life I live now, I find myself surrounded by these three incredibly entertaining boys. In all their grit and glory, they are mine, making memories, forming bonds, and many times either giving me a heart attack or grossing me out. I love them with all my heart. I love learning life through a boy's mind, and I love learning from them as much as I hope I am teaching them about the importance of a woman's heart.

Chapter 4

Times have changed

I CAN'T IMAGINE THAT I'M THE ONLY MOTHER WHO FEELS LIKE an outcast in the community. As I scroll Facebook, I see other parents getting together for lunch dates, dinner and drinks, and hanging out every weekend with other parents. I've never been part of that culture. Don't get me wrong, I live in a wonderful community filled with loving families and people who really care about our town, our school, and our kids. Looking back through my life, I've never really been part of the "in crowd." It's not who I am, it's not who I want to be, and it's not someone I will probably ever be. I'm a bit of a loner, a free spirit, a do-your-own-thing kind of gal, and that's just fine by me.

I don't like it when I feel that my kids are excluded out of certain situations or events because I'm not part of the clique. My children choose their friends; that does not mean I need to be friends with their parents, does it? I'm always friendly and kind to everyone I meet, but I have never felt the need to spend my weekends at restaurants and bars or in our neighbor's homes just to fit in with my children's friend's parents. When I was a kid, my parents would spend their weekends with us in our home or in our backyard. Occasionally, a couple of neighbors would stop by unannounced for a beer and munchies while all the kids played together. A big difference from how I grew up versus how my children are growing up is that the parents now get together a lot more often. Many parents today create their social lives around their children's friend's parents. When we were kids we spent more time as a family unit, not really interacting with other families. There were times when our neighbors would get together with us for a Saturday barbeque, but it wasn't a regular thing. My parents' way of life did not revolve around their own social needs, it revolved around their kids, their extended family, and time spent at home with all the kids. Honestly, we need more of that. Now, don't jump to conclusions and think I am antisocial. It's not that at all. All of my priorities have me as a parent first, doing parent things, loving and protecting my children, both emotionally and physically. It may sound old-fashioned to you, but if you stop and think about your own family, rather than create and attend social events for families to get together, why not create your own routines, your own activities, and your own special events with just your kids? You can tell them you love them a hundred times a day, but if you don't stop to spend time with them, your words won't mean much. It takes effort to be with your kids, but believe me, your actions will not go unnoticed. Start planning today how you can strengthen your bond with your kids by letting them know you enjoy their company.

I was recently at one of my kid's flag football games and over-heard a father boast about his parenting skills. "I am obsessed with knowing where my child is at every moment." While that sounds good and a responsible thing to do, all I could think about was that this father is in for a long, stressful journey of raising kids. I certainly agree that it is important to know where our children are and who they are with, but his use of the word *obsessed* concerned me. Obsession becomes a compulsion. A compulsion becomes something you cannot control. Now, I'm not obsessed with spying on my children and knowing every detail. I am hopeful that they make the right choices and that I have taught them through example to make good decisions and be safe. I firmly believe that part of being a kid is making mistakes and part of being a parent is being okay with knowing that that my kids will make mistakes. At the end of the day, all I really want is for my children to not harm themselves or someone else, and to be happy.

We can't protect our children from every situation, every hurt feeling, or every bit of danger. What we can do is teach them how to handle all of the things that life is going to throw at them, without becoming bitter. Adolescence is essentially the process of trial and error by trying new things, making mistakes, learning, and moving forward with a better understanding of life. Those are really the important lessons all people need to take out of all life's little bumps. Basically, learning to embrace the SUCK. As a parent, it's unreasonable to be obsessed with knowing every part or every minute detail of your child's life. It will drive you crazy and in time, it may create a wedge between you and your children. You wanting to know everything about your kids make them want to hide things from you. Once they reach a certain age, they want autonomy and they want you to trust them. You must accept that they have secrets. The truth is, as your kids get older, they experience more things that they are going to need to work out on their own. I feel pretty lucky because up to this point, my children are pretty honest with me. I know when they had their first kiss, I know when they got into a little trouble at school, and I know all the little things in between. I'm not foolish enough to think that I know everything that happens, and I'm sure there is plenty I will find out later in life. Frankly, I don't want to - or need to - know every detail of their struggles, it's part of being a kid, and it's my job to give them room to grow. All of this helicopter parenting is not good for our children, and it's not good for us. I joke about how I raise my children like it's still 1970, and others give me a funny look. The truth, is we should all be living a little bit more like it's 1970. Back then, kids were forced to think for themselves. They knew their place in front of adults, they knew they were the children and the adults were in charge. In the 70s, as kids, while we feared authority, we understood that they were there to take care of us, but not hover over every move we made. Today, many parents are creating a culture where we enable our children and force them to have the expectation that we are going to always be there to fix it and make it right. Although that is part of our job as parents, it is not our job to complete projects and make our children look better than their actual capabilities. That's not parenting, that enabling. I find it completely ridiculous. *For fuck sake,* put down that glue gun and step away from the project that's due tomorrow that your kid waited until the last minute to finish! All of these overly hands-on parents who take over every school and extra-curricular activity that are meant for their children is simply absurd. This is why we are also stressed. Our grown-up asses are participating in second grade science fairs, relearning math, and being obsessed with every move our children make. Not this girl.

One of the most obvious ways parents have changed is how much more they are involved in their kid's school work. There are certainly some good parts about this, but *for fuck sake*, stop doing your kids' class projects. Walking down the hallway during the elementary school science fair and seeing volcanoes erupt, ice glaciers melt, and all sorts of unbelievably constructed projects make me want to gag. You can always tell which projects are from the Morandi kids. They are sloppy, plain, and age-appropriate because they created them WITHOUT HELP from me or their dad. I refuse to sit down with any of my children to do any of their work. Not book reports, not science projects, and not even math homework. And speaking of math, when did 2 + 2 become an entire word problem that takes 20 minutes to complete? Our school even offered a Saturday class for parents to learn new math. Ummm.... no thanks. If you want to change math and teach it to my children, then rock on, but I'm simply not doing it. I'll take my chances and survive life knowing that 2 + 2 = 4, period. Call me a dunderhead, it's where I draw the line in the sand. It's just not happening.

I'm a mom, a real down and dirty mom. I like all the little things about being a mom. I like cleaning up the messes and listening to my kids tell their long, drawn-out stories about laughing when someone made a fart noise in class that day. I would rather listen to silly fart noise stories than try to keep up with the hair and the nails, makeup, name brand purses and all the forced ambitions that circulate in my small, little suburban town. I am the outcast. The one without many social friends in the community. I have no desire to be out with the other moms. It's like pretending we are friends, when actually it's just our kids who are friends. Mothers – get it right, not everyone wants to hang out with you. I'm sorry if I hurt your feelings. It's never about the social scene for me. It's always about the sports experience for my child. Frankly, Saturday nights are reserved for my family. I don't want to be out drinking, I want to be home with my kids and my husband doing mom things. Sounds weird, doesn't it? That's because it's just not that way anymore. Parents are so much more socially active than I ever remember my own parents being. They are out with other couples and living busy lives. Maybe they think they need it because, well, life's a bitch sometimes... and parents just wanna have fun. Now, *For Fuck Sake* isn't a book about whining; our society is what it is. It's a book about why I believe so many of us feel bullied into fitting into an unrealistic way of life when it comes to raising children in today's world.

This book is my attempt, and my perspective, to figure out how to raise children in a society that is competitive and chaotic at times because of over-stressing, over-scheduling, over-analyzing, and over-evaluating. My hope is that when other parents read this book, they will identify with the chaos and find a more peaceful and calm way to exist. We are all multitasking because we are so busy. If only we can learn the skill of *being present*. And yes, it is a skill. Being present for all the little moments, to learn how to appreciate the small details of life and be satisfied with our own parenting, while realizing some of it is downright mundane.

Meanwhile in the core of my soul, I want to raise children who are happy, who are whole, who feel safe, and who don't feel the stress of the world on their shoulders. I can't help but to wonder what happened to our society, what happened to us when we became parents. In fact, what happened to us as a nation? We have been brainwashed into believing that our children need to be at the top of the class, to be the most popular, the most athletic, or the most involved in extracurricular activities in order to be deemed successful in life. Well, *for fuck sake,* that is simply not true.

Raising kids in today's society like it's still 1970 is no easy task. We have reached the point where we now call other parents to create "play dates" so that our children can play together (it's a trap). We need to schedule appointments for just about everything, both for school and sports. It all seems so ridiculous. Remember when your parents said, "Be home when the street lights come on!" Well, I raise my kids where they still play outside until 9 o'clock at night, their feet are always dirty, their socks are always smelly, their hands are always grimy, and their bellies are always full. And they are happy. How do I know they are happy? I pay attention to the little things. I watch. I listen. I keep my distance when I need to, and I give hugs all the time.

In the age of the tiger moms, soccer moms, and baseball moms, I just want to be a mommy mom. A kind mom, a fun mom, a loving mom, a happy mom, and most importantly, a *present* mom. But I find myself alone when I am surrounded by so many seemingly overachieving moms, trying to keep up with efforts to keep up with what they perceive they need to keep up with. Oh, *for fuck sake*. I know there are many great moms out there who are regimented and what I consider overdoing and overachieving moms, but I question their intentions. I'm sure it's out of love, but is it because we are conditioned to think we have to enable our children in order to feel like we're doing is right? I suppose years from now, when they are all grown and raising their own children, we will find out. There is no question about it, being a mom can be lonely, scary, uncertain. and sometimes downright daunting, but all of it – every bit of it – is so incredibly rewarding.

I have an idea. I would like to start a grassroots movement where moms like me don't feel bullied into thinking that they are not enough, that their kids are not enough, and that their family is not enough because they are not overscheduled, overstressed, and overachievers. I want moms (and dads) to start taking back control of themselves and their families and (as important) their own peace of mind. In the long run our kids will be better, happier, and healthier. They will do just fine in life knowing they are cared for, they are loved, and just being who they are is enough. As I have grown as a mom, I have fully learned that you don't get any of these moments back; and you don't get a second chance to make the same mistake. I challenge you to hold on to each glorious moment, loving all the small moments and cherishing this season in life, for they will not last forever.

Chapter 5

What A Crock

I HAVE A SAYING: *IT'S ALWAYS THE SAME STORY WITH DIFFER-ent characters, and the different characters are the moms and dads and children.* Most people do it. Many define family differently, many bring customs, habits, and traditions into the family for years of great childhood memories. Even the insanity of child-rearing currently going on across our country has unique qualities, but, parenting is parenting, and it ends up all being the same. At the end of the day, parents everywhere have at least thought, *Oh, for fuck sake* a half a dozen time for many reasons; everything from messes, to behavior, to scheduling, to Internet time, to TV time, to who's cleaning the dishes and who's putting them away, and *for fuck sake* who's in the bathroom now? Are you feeling overwhelmed? Exhausted?

No, this is not a commercial. It is a public service announcement from me to you: It doesn't have to be that way.

The term, *for fuck sake* probably goes through my mind at least a dozen times a day. These three simple words help relieve any stress that may be building in me or the situation.

And this is how it started. In 2009, I just finished taking my children school shopping at one of the largest malls on Long Island. Going to the mall with four kids is like going on a field trip. Rule # 1 (the only rule): Be prepared for anything. Shopping for kids' clothes is fun for everyone. They all get something and we all go home happy! On that spectacular day, the kids were well-behaved and I was enjoying the experience. I felt proud of myself for handling this field trip with finesse! In tow, I was managing my children, ages 6, 4, 2 years, and a 2-months, alone, with no help – at the biggest mall in Long Island. *Pat me on the back!* I was feeling pretty impressed with myself. Not many mothers would do that, and not have it end up a disaster. To celebrate our new clothes and great behavior, we stopped at the food court. Even though food court food is not the best, after our day of success we were now in celebration mode! Once we got everything from all the different fast-food options, we sat down to eat with still no problems, and I'm still patting myself on the back for a job well done.

And there we were. I had all our packages, baby carriers, a stroller, and the just-purchased food surrounding the table with all the kids, when a nice old lady came by to tell me how well-behaved my children were. That moment was big for me. I was thinking, *Yes, I can do this!* I'm glowing, I'm proud, I'm feeling like I'm a total rock star, admiring my work of art and giving myself that extra pat on my back. But things changed quickly when Benjamin, my two-year-old, drops a French fry.

The woman innocently gestured with her hands and joked to him in that sing-songy voice old ladies use, "No more, all gone!"

To this day, I cannot explain why the next event took place. Benjamin, sitting there in his stroller, reached down to grab one of his navy-blue crocks from his foot. Then he looked up at the old lady as she was stooping down, and without warning, grabbed his shoe and bopped her right on the head. Yup, he full-fledged bopped the old lady on the head with his little blue crock for mocking him. I was mortified. A bad ending to an amazing day at the mall. But you know, I also learned that I should expect the unexpected. I was completely amused at myself because I thought I had my shit together. Yes, my friend. It was one of those moments that you end up saying in your head, *Oh, for fuck sake*. Little did I know then, that the term *for fuck sake* would be my mantra while raising my kids.

In our house, every school day is a surprise party. It's the moment where my kids truly have the look of, "Really? I have to get up? I have to get dressed? I have to eat breakfast, brush my teeth, get out the door by 6:45 in order to be on time? Again?" Every day they are surprised by this, even though this happens EVERY. SINGLE. MORNING. Frankly, it's mind-boggling.

I am up and functioning with them. I am in the kitchen cleaning up their messes while I watch them frantically run around the house, getting everything together. It's my morning ritual. I'm there to keep it calm, keep it moving, get everyone where they need to be with minimal stress. Every morning from 6:45 - 9:15 I'm in the midst of a circus and it's more exhausting than running a marathon. I know, because I've run in a lot of them. Every morning it is the same chaos, the same frantic behavior. And I am in the eye of the storm, watching my kids pull it all together. I'm not going to lie, I get a kick out of it. Every day - same story, same chaos, same thing. When I get them all to where they need to be I return to my home, and I clean up what they left behind. But before I start cleaning up the disaster, I look around, shake my head, and say with a smile, *Oh, for fuck sake.*

And then there are the awkward cocktail parties.

My husband, Peter, can walk into a room, mingle with people he may not know, and feel completely comfortable. He knows how to work a room and engage in small talk with strangers. I, on the other hand, feel completely lacking when talking to strangers. I want to crawl out of my own skin and hide in the corner. Dressed in uncomfortable heels, itchy dresses, and too much makeup, I feel like a little girl dressed up in her mother's clothing. I play it off well and I don't think anyone has any idea how uncomfortable I really feel. I am a friendly person but when I am put in a formal situation, I feel like a preteen at a school dance. The truth is, all I want to do is take the tray of hors d'oeuvres, find a corner to cower in, and stuff my face. Instead, I smile politely, chew slowly, and count the hours until I am in my pajamas curled up with a cup of tea and the latest book I'm reading.

I admire those who can feel so comfortable in social situations when they don't know many of the other people who are there. They know how to make small talk, to gesture correctly, and show others they are interested in them. I think it's an art to be able to attend parties and mingle with strangers so effortlessly. I believe many would view me as friendly and would find it hard to believe that I struggle with mingling with people I do not know. I see my own children act shy, quiet, and even standoffish. But get them home and they are outgoing, incredibly funny, obnoxiously loud, and have no problem talking about what's on their minds. Yet something about being outside the comfort of their own home makes them behave differently, just like I do. Of course, there are times when we have all been out in public and I have thought to myself, *for fuck sake* stop acting so weird. And then, I remind myself of the 'me' at those cocktail parties. I'm friendly, I say hello and I can be quite charming, yet I'm not being my true self. I am more reserved and a bit more unsure of my surroundings while trying to engage in casual conversation. It's the same thing with my children when they are outside our home, they are nothing like what they are when they are home. At home, inhibitions and constraints are dropped and they can be their true selves. In the comfort of our home my children are incredible witty, unbelievably interesting, and when it's time to talk serious, they have intelligent conversations ranging from politics to world events, and yes, even what's trending in social media. Times like these, I remind myself that when I get embarrassed and thinking *for fuck sake* and I try to act normal, they just may feel as weird as me when I'm at a cocktail party. I respect that. Not everyone enjoys the cocktail party for the party, they are there for the cocktails and hors d'oeuvres.

My children have taught me that I cannot make them who I want them to be, or behave how I want them to behave, or like the things that I like. While our ego dictates that our children are ours; truth is, my children are their own people and I have very little control over their authentic selves. In fact, as parents, none of us have control over a lot of things.

Now, let's just ponder that idea for a minute. Take the subject of laundry. In expecting the unexpected, there are times I have no control. Why is it that every time I wash my kids' sheets and put them back on their beds, that same night someone manages to wet them? Why does this happen time and again? Is it Murphy's Law? Is God playing a joke? Are the laundry gods wanting a little extra attention? It's just not mathematically possible to have as much laundry as I do. Once when they were clean, I couldn't wait to hop into bed for the evening. Eventually, I learned that my son, Matthew, liked them, too. One evening he climbed into my bed and wanted to snuggle with me, but he fell asleep. Instead of moving him into his bed that night, I decided to let him stay there. Mistake number one. Between the kicks and the nonstop nighttime restlessness, I barely slept. Finally, around 2 a.m. he woke me up, announcing that he was going to go into his own bed. I asked why, and he said, "Because I just peed in your bed and I want to sleep in my bed." It is true. We all like clean, dry sheets.

Now, think what you want, but I have been peed on my fair share of times, and to have my child unabashedly imply that it was not his problem and his own bed was dry so he was going there, literally cracked me up. I laughed myself back to whatever sleep I could get before morning. My kids never cease to amaze me. I'm just saying that sometimes *for fuck sake*, all you can do is laugh.

One year when all four children were small, we ventured off for a family getaway to the Dominican Republic. It is a tradition to always make a care package for the kids to enjoy on the plane for our trip. I do it just about every time we travel. Whether a car ride or a plane ride, they always had a bag full of goodies to keep them occupied, happy, and quiet. Because Matthew was barely a year old, I made a special care package for him with lots of treats and things he liked and could munch on. I guess his stomach wasn't feeling so well and at his young age, he really couldn't tell me. After he ate all the snacks, there was an incredible explosion beyond an explosion in his diaper. ON. THE. PLANE. To my incredibly embarrassing horror, everyone around us started grabbing barf bags and putting stuff over their faces to avoid the revolting smell. To give you an idea of what we were dealing with, the small aircraft had a tiny bathroom, so trying to clean a baby covered in shit and changing him into a clean diaper was a challenge. If ever there was a *for fuck sake* moment, this was it. I tried my best to clean up as I was doing this, and with the help of some worried airline stewardesses, we used napkins and rags and did our best to wash him down. No matter how hard I tried to avoid it, I was literally covered in shit. We were 60,000 feet in the sky in a small plane, and I was the stinky, shitty-smelling lady grossing everyone out. And they knew it. All I could do was laugh because I knew that there was nothing I could have done to make the situation better or make anyone on the plane more comfortable. Sometimes, literally, shit just happens!

Most of growing up is having experiences that lead to lessons learned. I hope that when my kids think back on all the lessons they have learned, they know to apply them in their adult lives. When Emma was born, I was so thrilled to have a daughter. My first child was a boy, and it was a nice balance to bring a daughter into our world. As a child growing up, she was always dressed in pink with bows and bonnets and she would always proudly dance around the house looking adorable as ever. I always called her my little lady because she took such pride in being a girl, with all the wonderful gifts that it brings.

One late afternoon we were visiting my mom in upstate New York. It had been raining for most of the day and Emma was entertaining herself by walking arounds the grounds and inspecting every little flower or bug that she came across. She has always been the type of girl to stop and explore the beauty of nature and enjoy all the magnificent elegance that surrounds her. There she was in her adorable green and pink dress with her matching pink shoes and matching bonnet with her little pigtails so perfectly placed on each side of her head. I admired her from afar and commented to my husband how captivating she was to watch. Once she saw us, she happily skipped over to our direction, and in doing so fell face first straight into a massive mud puddle. There lay my beautiful two-year-old baby girl literally stuck in the mud. I will be honest with you. Peter and I laughed so hard that neither of us moved to help her out of the mud. She finally picked herself up and trudged her way toward us, both mortified and outraged that we found such humor at her expense. To this day, when I think of her stuck in the mud, it still makes me laugh. Now, she wasn't hurt, just dirty and muddy and funny looking. I found the words to explain my thoughts to her: No matter how beautiful you may feel or whatever beauty may surround you, there will always be a pile of mud trying to muck it up for you. My message to Emma is the same message I tell my boys. It is up to you to pick yourself up out of the mud and come through the puddle to dry land. Sometimes you may feel paralyzed, sitting in the mud, but you must find a way to continue on. Through time, you learn to jump over the puddle or just stand up, brush yourself off, and go forward. Every time you brush yourself off it becomes easier and easier.

Everyday tasks can often feel just as overwhelming. For me, food shopping is exhausting. Necessary, but exhausting. You drive there, look for a parking spot, get your shopping cart, then navigate yourself through over-stimulating aisles and aisles of groceries. Persevering through every aisle, deciding on options, looking for healthy kid snacks, banking on the best prices is a skill I try to master each time I am shopping, despite the fact that I find the entire experience hellish.

Pushing an overflowing cart, filled with food for a week, maneuvering up and down aisles with a bunch of strangers or 'friends' I don't want to run into, then trying to make my way to the cash register, hoping not to knock down the end display or run over that old person bending down is not an easy feat. Then I have to unload the cart that I just spent a couple of hours painstakingly filling with stuff. When the transaction is done and after my eyes pop out of my head at the cost to feed four growing children, I roll the cart out to the car, load up the car, and head home, hoping there is someone there to help unload and put away. Guess what? No one's home. Not yet. The Fab Four will start rolling in soon, but I can't wait for that. Mixing one havoc with another havoc can be a bit too much, so I take in the grocery bags myself and put everything away in its right spot. No part of this entire experience is fun for me, but it happens every week, and it is a special moment for the kids when they come home and open all the cabinets to see what I bought.

I take a pause at the kitchen table after everything is put away. Then like clockwork, those children of mine, who could not be found just moments ago, suddenly appear from everywhere, and so do their friends. They start rummaging through the cabinets and fridge and become engrossed in consuming all of the food and drink they can manage. All of my careful organizing and arranging of newly bought food quickly becomes a vast chaotic mess of deliciousness.

I stand there speechless. I am in awe of how quickly and how much kids can eat, and I am forever grateful that my house is filled with healthy children who I am able to nourish. As quickly as they arrived, they were gone. I am left with empty wrappers, sticky counters, and happy kids. Suddenly I realize. *Oh, for fuck sake!* I need to go to the store tomorrow. Gotta stock up on the breakfast bars! For a minute I am annoyed, but I am happy and grateful that I have these little annoyances in my life to enjoy. One day I know I will have a clean house, with no wrappers left around, no laundry baskets to empty, and everything will be forever tidy. I know that I will look back on these days and miss them. I know that I will long for them, and my heart will hurt for them, but for now, I want to live in the present. So, I continue my every other day trips to the grocery store, spending hundreds of dollars on snacks, a ridiculous amount of time shopping, and expending an overwhelming amount of energy in the process. No matter how many times I do this, the chatter in my head says *for fuck sake* and the love in my heart says give me more.

For as many *for fuck sakes* as there are, there are so many more precious moments that I wouldn't trade for the world. Moments that I hold close to me are ones I always carry so that when I'm older I can sit in my rocking chair and remember when I had the privilege to watch my family grow.

Raising a family in today's world is never going to be easy, but it will always be worth it. At the end of the day, I don't regret the decisions I made to give up my career and stay home to raise my children. It was best for me, it was best for my children, and it was best for my family. While I am not leading the life of what others would expect from a college graduate, I am happy, I am whole, and I know I am doing what is right for me by living my own truth. There is no shame in being a stay-at-home mom and there's no shame to have your children be your number one priority. When you put family first, everything falls into place. It's easy to talk the talk, but very few walk the walk. Are you talking? Or are you walking?

Now more than ever it's time for Americans to take a stand and get our family back in order. Forget about the nonstop sports commitment, forget about going out with other adult friends, it doesn't matter about your designer bag or clothes or the car you're driving. What will always matter at the end of the day is your children and your family and all the wonderful memories and glorious times you had with them. You cannot get this time back and the older you get, the more you will realize how much you will yearn for the small little incidences that seemed so minor at the time. For me, through the process of raising my children I have come to realize just how precious life was when they were small, innocent, and unafraid.

So, this is my idea. All this chaos is just a season. A short, crazy, rewarding season of life. This is the season where you understand true commitment, love, perseverance, and the desire to never give up. What's important is that you must show up every day. On the good days, but especially on the bad days (and there *are* bad days), you just have to show up. Part of parenting is that you have to keep trying, keep motivating, and keep finding the energy and unconditional love to move onward. With so much information overload on what's the right way to raise kids, even the best parents question themselves. We wonder, are we pushing hard enough? Are we pushing too much? Do we show enough love? Do we give enough discipline? Are we doing it right? My advice is pure and simple. Show love: as much, as freely, and as often.

Believe me, when you show love, the rest has a way of working itself out in the most glorious ways.

Chapter 6

Bamboozled

PART OF LIFE IS THAT SOMETIMES YOU GET BAMBOOZLED. Sometimes it is in business, sometimes it is by friends or family, and many times it is by your own children. I have fallen for so many phony stories, exaggerated truths, and misleading circumstances, I can't even begin to count. It always leaves me shaking my head and chuckling.

One early afternoon, I received a call from the elementary school telling me that my seven-year-old was ill and needed to be picked up. I was in the middle of food shopping and dropped everything because Benjamin rarely complained or went to the nurse. That meant he was feeling pretty lousy. When I got there, his little body was laying down on the small cot behind a curtain. I bent down close to his ear and whispered, "Hi bud. How are you feeling?" His big brown eyes looked over at me and he seemed weak. He was sad. "Not so good." I rubbed his forehead long enough for him to give me a wink and a thumb's up. I started to chuckle because it was an absurd moment, and I was now involuntarily in on this scam. I quickly filled out the paperwork and left the school with Benjamin before we were questioned any further. Once in the car, I confronted my son.

"Benjamin, tell me. What just happened there?" My voice was steady, and honestly, deep down I knew that if my kid trusted me to be a participant in his scheme, I would probably not have a problem with that.

In his small squeaky voice, he boastfully responded, "Gotcha! Now, where are we going? Ice cream? Park? Hike? You name it, and I'm in!" Now here is my precious little seven-year -old boy, planning and plotting all on his own in order to pull off a *Gotcha!* That was pretty brave of him to think that I would go along with it… or willing enough to take the punishment if the whole thing goes south in a hurry. Truth is, I was so grateful to spend the afternoon with him, and to this day, I laugh about how it was planned.

I know. By now you are probably shaking your head and uttering tsk, tsk! I get that you may think Benjamin deserved a punishment. For the record, Benjamin and I talked about it at length. He had a one-time pass. We both reached an understanding. But to be honest with you, the best thing that came out of that entire episode was the realization that one day in school, my precious seven-year-old was thinking about his mommy and came up with a pretty creative way to beat the system and make that happen for him. Can't fault a son for doing that, can you?

I never dreamed in a million years that I would get a dog. I see people treat their dogs like family members, and I never quite understood it. In fact, if anyone would ask me about my biggest fear, I would say dogs. I know it's silly, but growing up, I truly had a tremendous amount of fear of dogs, kind of like how people have a fear of snakes or scorpions or killer bees. I know it's not rational, but it was a true fear of mine. When a dog would come close to me, my palms would become sweaty and I would get very nervous. Sometimes I wonder if maybe in a past life I was attacked by killer dogs or something. In any case, I swore I would never get a dog. After four children, why would I want to take care of another living thing? I used to say I don't even want to take care of a house plant, so I certainly don't want to pick up dog poop, go to vet visits, or wake up in the wee hours of the morning for yet another living thing. But my family didn't want to hear that.

The kids would make up songs and stories and draw pictures of them getting a dog. They were relentless, laying it on thick. They tried to convince me that I would ruin their entire childhood if they didn't get a little creature of their own. Like people all over America, we eventually gave in to the begging, pleading, and crocodile tears: We got our children a dog. For me, it came at a very emotional time in my life. My children were two, four, six, and eight. A very close uncle of mine was in the ICU, suffering from diabetes. He was young, and it was heartbreaking to watch my cousins go through the same sadness I experienced, of watching their father dying. Around the same time my beloved grandmother, the woman who was truly a friend to me, passed away. I was devastated by the loss, and it is still remains as one of the biggest losses of my life. Meanwhile, my cousin was caring for her four-year-old son who was just diagnosed with a brain tumor. Here I was with my four healthy children, and our biggest problem was them pleading for a dog that I did not want. Yet all around me, people I cared a lot about were suffering. In a split-second decision, I announced, "C'mon kids, let's go get a dog!" I convinced myself that they would hold their promises of feeding, walking, and picking up the poop. I was in such denial that my children – at their very young age – would do anything but keep their end of the bargain. Of course, the first day we got our dog, we fell in love instantly. That first night when we brought him home, Rusty kept running back and forth in our kitchen like a crazy dog and I didn't know how to handle it. My fear took hold of me and I jumped up on one of the chairs, scared to come down to care for this six-pound puppy. In the beginning, I was terrified of Rusty. It seems silly now to think that this small adorable puppy made me so nervous, while having four children came so naturally and without fear.

Rusty is now such an important part of our family and is a trusted friend and companion. I can't imagine not having him around. And yes, as it turns out, I'm the one to feed, and walk Rusty, although I did somehow manage to get Emma to keep her end of the bargain about cleaning up the poop. Small victories.

I would never define myself as gullible, but I do have a big heart and assume that people have the same love and good intentions that I do. Unfortunately, I have been proven wrong in the past, but those times have not jaded me; I am just more cautious now. One day at the grocery store I couldn't help but notice a man lingering on the street corner. He was holding a sign that read, "please help." I was drawn to him. I'm not sure why, but I felt a sense of sadness come over me. He seemed to have kind eyes, so I started talking to him. I was shocked at what I learned. He was a little down on his luck and didn't have enough money to pay all of his rent. He admitted he wasn't homeless, but he just didn't have enough at the end of every month to pay his bills and put food on the table for himself and his wife.

I cannot fully explain what came over me, except that my gut and my heart guide a lot of my choices. I guess you could say that I befriended this man. I started bringing him water and food and I would sit with him and chat while he ate. I remember one day in particular where I sat on the curb with him and got to get to know him a little better. In my heart, I thought I was doing the right thing. I continued with our friendship month after month, where I would bring him some water and food, and he would sit and talk with me. Some people thought I was crazy. In fact, one man driving his shiny new Audi stopped where we were seated and started yelling at me, saying that I was part of the reason for the homeless invading our neighborhood.

As it turned out, he admitted he had his own set of money woes, even though he drove an Audi. He argued that no one gives him hand-outs, and he knows what he has to do to get himself out of his mess and he is working on it. He added that it just wasn't fair. This guy I'm feeding is doing nothing by taking a handout. I told this gentleman that it was my choice to be there, and I didn't have to answer to him. I feel strongly about living my own truth, not someone's perception of me. I have faith that God has put me here to help and serve others. This man had no business injecting his opinion.

In my *Aha!* moment, I realized that so many people, all around us, are going through all sorts of challenging situations and that life does not always appear to be what it seems. I continued bringing this man food, talking to him, and being kind. Then one day, without warning, he was gone. Months later, when I was in my local Walgreens getting some pictures developed, I noticed him. He looked far different than the man that I spent so much time sitting on the curb with, providing food for and speaking with him. He was dressed in a nice jersey and clean jeans. His hair was slicked back, and he was carrying two cartons of cigarettes and a case of beer. I took a pause. I just didn't know if this man's luck had changed or he simply, cleanly, and stealthily bamboozled me. If he conned me out of food and water and some conversation, then that's the chance I took. Truth be told, I have absolutely no regrets. In any case, it didn't stop me from helping others when I can. If anything, I now pause for a minute, give myself a gut check, and continue to be there for those in need. For as many *for fuck sakes* there are, there are also people who do need help from strangers. I'm hoping that the man's luck changed and he was gaining ground, but my gut tells me that I may have been deceived. I think it was the two cartons of cigarettes and the case of beer.

Being generous is something that is important to me. When my kids were younger, I felt it was important to teach them about giving back to those in need. Every so often, we would go through all of our closets and drawers and get rid of things that no longer fit or that we simply no longer wanted. One time in particular, with all four kids in tow, we went to the goodwill store to drop off our stuff. As soon as we walked in, Emma announced to everyone, "Okay, so we have the good Will, which one in here is the bad Will?"

At five years old, her perspective of goodwill was that her brother, whose name is William, was, in fact, the "good Will," and that somewhere in that store there had to be a "bad Will." Everyone laughed and

Emma didn't get it, but it was still a wonderful experience for my kids. I dropped off the stuff we collected from home, and as I was pulling away from the Goodwill store, I remember shaking my head and thinking, *oh, for fuck sake,* you can never predict what will come out of the mouths of babes.

Speaking of the good will/bad will, there is no one on Earth who can make me laugh like my William. This child is witty, sharp, and sarcastic, and yet one of the nicest people I have ever known. That being said, he is always looking for an angle. I suppose much of it is age appropriate, but he can make something bad seem very good. On any random day, we will walk in the house with such joy and announce, "C'mon Ma, high five me! Right here, Ma. Right here..." He says this before telling me what amazing thing happened at school that day. I always high five back and then ask why. With eyes wide open and a smile from ear to ear, William proudly asks, "Guess who got a 72 on his math test? That's right... THIS guy!"

"Wait. What? Did I just high five a 72?" And then he slips away as smoothly as he slipped in. We both know that I'm not pleased with a 72, but he found a way to pull it off so confidently that there was nothing else to do but laugh. My son knew the meaning of "strategy." There was another time when I began to notice that William kept missing homework assignments, so I requested that he show them to me each night. The first night he shows me a piece of paper, I nod, say good job, and he goes upstairs. The second day he again comes to me with his homework, I glance at it and say, "Good, William, glad to see you are doing your homework." He walked away with a smirk and a shrug. The next day when he came to me again, I happen to look more closely at his assignment. And then it hit me. This was the same piece of paper he had waved in front of me the last three days. When I questioned him about it, he just chuckled, and said, "*Gotcha!*" I was left standing there in the kitchen amused and dumbfounded. William has a gift for making the ridiculous seem sane. To be honest, it's part of his charm, his DNA, (and I think he got it from me). You just can't help but to love this kid.

With all of the humor my oldest child brings, he has also learned the lesson of "don't piss on a hornet's nest." When William was a little boy we were upstate at my mom's house and while he was playing in the woods nearby, he had to pee. Like any young boy, he could not hold it long enough to get back to the house and had no problem peeing in the woods. Like most little boys, it's an honor and a freedom to pee outside. Where he stood was where he went. Unfortunately, unbeknownst to him, there was an underground hornets' nest, and up came a dozen bees stinging his ankles, and his knees, and all the way to... well, you know.

William learned a lot that day, and from that experience he is now aware of his surroundings and always knows that at any unexpected moment something can come up and sting you without warning. As much as my son thinks he can manipulate me, he has also learned that if you are not careful, life will come back and sting you in the wanker.

Chapter 7

Don't Judge, I'm Judging

WHAT EVER HAPPENED TO MOM PANTS? THAT WAS A THING, right? It was a way to tell the moms from their teenage daughters. Now when I look around, every mother I see is dressed like their 16-year-old. It's all so confusing. Mom pants may not have been the most attractive thing, but it was less confusing and it put all moms on an equal playing field. Ridiculous "comfy" outfits distinguished the moms from the ridiculously uncomfortable non-moms. Can you imagine now, showing up to a school function in mom's jeans, a holiday sweater, and wearing a pair of Keds? Would never happen. I want mom jeans back!

Almost all the woman around me have their hair, makeup, nails and outfits so damn near perfect that I feel like I am in high school all over again. I see them at the grocery store. I see them standing in line at the post office. Going to Starbucks. Getting gas for their cars. I see them dropping their kids off to school. *Oh, for fuck sake, you're not even getting out of the car!*

Still insecure and unsure of the latest fashion and almost certain that I have already missed out on what's trending, I look around and I can spot all the moms; There are the sassy- dressed moms, the moms that think they are still twenty moms, the sporty moms, the all about the school team moms, the tanned moms, the breast implanted moms, the business professional moms… and then you have me, the mom who doesn't give a rat's ass and it shows. I am who I am and in the scheme of things, it doesn't matter if I don't "fit in." In the morning, I drive my kids to school in my pajamas. Then I generally spend my mornings in workout gear, and if I want to really fancy myself up, I tie my hair in pigtails, put on a sundress, wear *way* too much pink lipstick, and call myself dressed and ready to go! I'm a self-proclaimed disaster, but I play it off as part of my charm. Not sure if that's working or not.

I want to be honest with you right here and now. I consider myself a hands-off parent when it comes to school projects. It's a lonely feeling. I remember once, walking down the school hallway during Emma's second grade science fair, inspecting each student project with skepticism and disdain. There were flowing volcanos, windmill experiments, elaborate technology experiments, and incredibly (over-my head) scientific analysis with full theories and conclusions. When I got to Emma's project of "Which fruit roll up tastes the best?" I looked at the scribbled oak tag paper with immense pride. Unlike many of the other mothers there, I was in awe of my daughter's project. Unlike all of the mothers who were there, hoping for first or second place for their child, I was STILL in awe of what my amazing second grader did for the science fair. You go, Emma!

Science fairs are tricky because kids are the ones receiving the honor, yet the secret code among many adults is that they were there to help their child. Now, I would proofread and even cut out some stuff for my child, if asked to do so, but other than that, I am hands off. When I do assist in small ways, it gives me a chance to spend some time with my kids, listening to them explain to me what they intend to do. I've been through 4 science fairs times 8 grades. I've got this down. Once I know what their project is, and if they need any specific supplies, I back away until they are ready to present it to me. Everything else is their hard work, their own ideas, and their fully ridiculous, yet innocent, non-scientific project.

Everyone, and I mean everyone: the student, the parent, the teacher, the principal, your neighbor, grandma, grandpa…well, you know what I mean… everyone knows what a 7- year-old child can do. It's that simple. So, now we have moms (and dads) inspecting other parent-made science fair projects, and in the process judging the work of other parents! How's that for absurdity? Just picture it. Moms wearing clothes that are too tight, too short, and too revealing are walking around, inspecting projects done by other moms who are wearing too tight, too short, and too revealing clothes. *Oh, for fuck sake*, this. is. just. a. children's. science. fair. Attention enabling parents: get over yourself. Wait, that sounds harsh, but at least give yourself (and your kids) a break. It's okay that your child hasn't cured cancer or knows how to solve world hunger yet. What is great is that they are able to come up with their own project, theory and conclusion on something age-appropriate - like the best tasting fruit roll up. My kids may not win any science award, but I would bet that they worked harder and longer on their projects than yours did. They spent more time thinking about their topic while they are creating it. They may have daydreamed or thought of other stuff they could be doing; but instead they were concentrating on getting the project done. I would like to think that through their bright little minds, they may have thought of bigger dreams, like inventing ways to measure data when finding the best tasting fruit roll-up. Helicopter parents do their children a disservice by always hovering inches away from every move their child makes. Let them think, make mistakes, draw their own conclusions, and *for fuck sake,* let them do their own school assignments. Just so you know, earlier I told you about my son, William, who waved the same homework assignment in front of me for three days. His math teacher dealt with him and he had consequences. William made a choice, and he had to own that. We all learn our lessons differently.

Even though I am not the helicopter parent, I know the importance of having my finger on the pulse of what's going on in my children's lives. I would say that I am the "behind the scenes" parent. I am definitely there if (and when) they need me, but I stand back and run the house. Four kids make for a lively family. Something's always going on. So, while I'm on the sidelines, so to speak, I am doing laundry, washing dishes, making dinner, going to work, doing some writing, carpooling, food shopping, and organizing just about everything else that makes our family run smoothly. Every once in a while, I get away to my favorite park to sit on the bench or run the course, taking in my moments alone, as I sift through each of my child's needs and prepare for the next day. Announcement: Parenting is 24/7. It's different from helicoptering and it's definitely different from being in the same room as your kids and gluing your eyes to the screen on your phone. News Flash: That's not parenting. But back to my kids.

On a typical day, they are all very casual and unassuming. They have very little care for what is going on around them except if there is milk in the fridge and if we have those three different varieties of chips they are craving. They don't notice the endless piles of laundry, the mounting dishes in the sink, the dinner burning in the oven, or the sticky (substance unknown) floors. They engage in conversation to ask if I picked up their favorite snack, and if I can drive them to their practice. They have no real concept of time, and as I run through the house to be where I need to be, at the time I need to be there, they mosey. They grab one more snack, another quick look in the mirror, and a last-minute change of clothes. As I struggle to put on my shoes, find my keys, and rush out the door, I am amazed how I am their time keeper. I am expected to make sure we are on time with very little effort or concern from their end. It's a position that I find daunting. To them, it just happens. There are four of them and only one of me, and many schedules to coordinate each crazy afternoon. And here I am, left juggling all these balls in the air with almost no wrinkles in their schedule. I do a pretty good job at this, they barely notice, if at all, that I'm completely frazzled and in way over my head. They have no idea what it takes to be me! I guess that is one of the talents of being a mother. I want it to be seamless for them. I don't want them to stress over these logistical things. There will be plenty of time to experience it when they get older. By then, I will have nurtured their critical thinking skills and taught them to just breathe, *for fuck sake.* No, I would never say that. But what I will do is be there, coaching them as they learn how to plan ahead and use their time wisely.

I will admit, there are times when I envy my kids' nonchalance – unaware of how intense the moment is for me to coordinate all this, as they stroll down the stairs, make that one last post on social media, and take one last selfie before we're out the door. As I am sitting in the car waiting for them to join me, they have no idea that there's a war going on with me and the time. I look at the clock, figuring out how long it will take if I make all the green lights. Reality is, we won't, so I settle on being a couple minutes late as one by one, each kid steps out of the house and finds their place in the car.

One of the benefits of being a kid to a mom like me is that I carry the stress and my kids carry the benefits. Most days we make it on time, but it's always close and I'm almost always yelling, "You're going to be late!" *Oh, for fuck sake,* the clock moves fast on my most busy days, and my kids move at kid speed, which is whatever speed they want.

Clearly, I am the self-proclaimed anti-helicopter parent, yet even I fall victim to protecting my precious babies at any cost. There have been a number of times when I could have let one of my children fail, but chose not to let that happen, just as there have been times I could have saved them from failing and did nothing. It depends on the situation and the circumstances for which way I will go. When it comes to these critical moments, I am calculating the pros and cons of me stepping in, and I carry my responsibility seriously. Like I mentioned earlier, parenting is 24/7.

My wake-up call occurred when Matthew was eight years old. I was busy cleaning up after breakfast and we were rushing to get out of the house. I asked him to go upstairs and put the clothes in the dryer for me. After a couple of minutes, he returned back downstairs and went about playing his game of checkers with his brother, Benjamin. Within a few minutes, it occurred to me that I hadn't heard the dryer actually go on, and asked Matthew if he turned it on when he put the clothes in it. He responded, "No you didn't tell me to do that. You only asked me to put the clothes in the dryer."

I thought that it would make sense to an 8-year-old that the wet clothes that he just put in the dryer needed to be dried. It surprised me that he did not know this. I never remember it coming up with the other three kids when they were his age. Surely, I must have told one of them to put the clothes in the dryer. But my youngest child, who knows how to use a smart phone, a computer, a laptop, and can figure out a math problem quicker and better than me, did not think to turn on the dryer once the wet clothes were in it. I obsessed over this new information for hours. I couldn't get it out of my head that a simple cause and effect concept – applied through critical thinking – was not being taught some way through learning subjects at school. Because I sure in hell wasn't teaching it at home. I kept thinking about what I could have done for Matthew to enforce this concept in his everyday living, and I found that I got better at explaining certain tasks. My children teach me things every day. That day was one of those days.

It is my job to make sure my children go out into the world with excellent common sense. Are we losing this because we are so used to telling our kids what to do, when to do it, and how to do it? I don't want that for my children. I want them to think for themselves and explore their own possibilities in understanding cause-and-effect. These are all such important lessons for our children to understand, and yet what students are learning in school sometimes isn't transferring to their real-world experience. My kids spend close to eight hours a day in a school environment. There's got to be more to it than teaching to the test and hoping for high scores. I want more for my children. In fact, I demand it.

I don't have all the answers, but one thing I have learned from my children is how to have an open dialog with them. I have a reasonably open relationship with them and I think it's an important part of a mother and child partnership. Open relationships with my children have evolved over time, as I respect certain needs for privacy. But when it comes to the realities of teenage and tweener lives, my kids are not shy at all in telling me what's going on. They talk about everything from missing homework assignments in school, to what their teachers may have said, anything big that happened at school, arguments between friends, underage drinking by people they know, and even first kisses. I'm happy my kids feel comfortable with me to talk about their sometimes-confusing and fast-spinning world. I will never be one of those mothers who says *not my kid*, because I'm not that smug nor naïve to think that because it may not be my kids today, that doesn't mean it won't be my kids tomorrow. Sometimes teenage life happens, so I will never proclaim with 100 percent confidence that it won't be my kid. My ego tells me that trust in teenagers is just not that secure.

Ego dictates your life. Being over-scheduled in activities, over-zealous in science projects, and overly confident in your actions, your ego is bound to get in the way. EGO. Because we all feel the need to keep up, be the best, be the loudest, the most involved, and the busiest, our egos get in the way of what is really important day-to-day. That is, the growth of our children, the health of our family, and keeping our personal sanity. Now, we can't change everything, and we certainly can't change how others behave. We can, however, start with ourselves and our own children.

What kind of relationship do you have with your children? Do you push them into sports because you like baseball, and so your kid has to like it? Are you interfering with your child's school project because you believe she can have the very best one in the class (or at least second best)? This goes back to the ego issue. You want your child's project to be better than your neighbor's. I have said this before. It's not about you.

Learn when to step away. In doing so, you will not only help your children's self-esteem (and ego), it will make for a calmer family. Parents see me as sort of laid back, and unfazed by it all. They want to feel more relaxed as well. My answer is always yes, you can. I am all for being involved in my kid's life. I am always on the sidelines, sometimes watching, sometimes asking questions, and sometimes giving them praise for their good work. I remind myself that it is not about me. Yes, I too, have learned to get over myself.

You may be asking yourself, "Well, what makes her such an expert on this?" It's true, I'm not an expert. I can only tell you that I have 4 perfectly imperfect happy kids, and all of it works for me. It wasn't always that way. From all the lessons I learned from my children, the biggest one is don't let my ego get in the way.

I remember one unmistakable time that I didn't heed my own advice. When I was potty training my oldest son, William, I lost my cool when he had an accident. I went ballistic for 30 seconds and screamed at him, "Now I'm throwing away all of your spider-man underwear because you are a baby and you can't go on the toilet like other big boys do!" As soon as those words left my mouth, I wanted to stuff them way, way back in. There stood William with tears seeping out of his eyes and streaming down his little face. I felt ashamed. I was angry with myself and vowed never to do that again. It wasn't that he had an accident in his new underwear, it was that I let my ego get in the way. In my mind, he wasn't as far along as I thought he would be, and I let that fuel my anger and frustration. To date, that has been my biggest regret as a parent. I learned from it and vowed never to let my own ego get in the way of my child's happiness or growth.

I am not perfect. Being a parent is a work-in-progress. It never ends. For me, the key is to pay attention. More importantly, it is to learn from my mistakes. I want my kids to feel comfortable in their own skin and confident in who they are, but I also want to make sure that they are living up to their fullest potential. It's not always easy, and with four kids, I walk a tightrope on this point. I have one kid who is a complete overachiever and I wish she would relax a bit and another who needs a fire lit under his ass. The one thing that I am certain of is that they are going to be who they are going to be. I can influence, I can hope, I can demand, but at the end of the day, they are their own people and all that I truly wish for them is to be healthy, happy, and kind.

Chapter 8

Life Happens

THERE ARE TIMES THAT WE JUST FUCK UP. WE DON'T MEAN TO and we never intended to, but we're human, and sometimes we just mess it up. Even small infractions make us feel like we have failed the mother card. Just today, I was asked to drop off my oldest son's golf jersey for his team picture. I had it cleaned, folded and ready to go. I got stuck at the supermarket for three extra minutes, no exaggeration. The woman helping me was in a very chatty mood and in no rush to complete my order. Those three minutes cost my son his chance to be in the high school golf picture. It may not seem that big of a deal, and he wasn't all that upset, but I felt like shit. I dropped the ball and it was a terrible outcome. Ouch. But it happens. Sometimes even the best intentions don't turn out the way we plan.

In hindsight, mom moments are endearing. In real time, mom moments can be humiliating. One particularly busy evening, I made my five-year-old daughter mac & cheese and as I was taking the hot water to the sink to dump out the boiling noodles, she came barreling right into me! I was caught off guard and spilled hot water all over her beautiful head. It was horrible, and the healing process took forever, which was a constant reminder that I caused that burn. Luckily, it caused no permanent damage to my daughter, but for me, I am emotionally scarred and I am not sure I will ever completely forgive myself for what happened.

Each of my two youngest boys cried a lot as an infant. It was different with the first two babies, but by the time my third child came around, I began to slow down. By child number 4, I was exhausted. They cried and never slept. We were up all night and I was on the constant go, go, go cycle. They each challenged every ounce of fortitude we had to serve their needs. We were there for them. At the time, I was feeling like Superwoman and felt I didn't need a lot of sleep, since I was on a schedule of little sleep and I was functioning okay. Or so I thought. I didn't realize what kind of fog I was in half the time. I'm sure a lot of mothers feel this way.

One especially busy day I was lucky because the angels were with me. I just came back from running errands and at the time my two-year-old and newborn child were buckled into their car seats. I pulled into the driveway and got out to unlock the front door. What I didn't do is put the car in park. Yes. I forgot to put the car in park. Horrified, I watched my car roll swiftly toward the gate, heading straight for the pool. As my vehicle continued rolling toward the fence, ripping it down in its fury, I knew that it was headed into the pool. I grabbed on to the car door and slammed on the brakes. The boys had no idea of the fear in my heart that day, and that is probably a blessing. The only damage done was to the fence that is around the pool. My babies were safe. I was so grateful, and I know that God was watching over us that day. It's something I will never forget. It took me a long, long time to forgive myself for that. I also know that not all mothers get lucky like I did on that day. In the end, everything turned out okay, minus a broken fence. The most important thing was that my babies were safe.

When my oldest child was around seven years old, I was completely and rightfully frazzled. I was basically caring for my four children alone, with little help from my husband who at the time was working hard to advance in his career. At the time, my kids ranged from the age of seven to a newborn. Each child is about 2 to 2 1/2 years apart from the next one. I was rushing off to a karate class for my oldest, something he didn't particularly enjoy much, but we were doing it, and trying to feed all of the children a snack before we got there. The mission was to get him there on time. They were still very young and were being forced to hurry up. The next thing I know, they started getting stressed and it made things worse.

It was mayhem, complete and utter mayhem. I screamed in their small little faces to rush to eat, chew, c'mon chew faster, hurry, so we can get to karate class on time. That was me: overwhelmed, and sleep deprived. Most times we learn a lesson right after an event occurs. This was that moment. Something changed. I made the decision that I would never live like that again. It was a pure, unadulterated *"aha!"* moment. *"Oh, for fuck sake, Donna,* the child is seven years old, he is not the fucking karate kid, get. over. yourself."* Sometimes you have to give yourself a wake-up call, give yourself a nudge, and say *for fuck sake* get hold of yourself, you're freaking out over nothing. It's not about you.

The moral here is that we are not perfect. No matter how good our intentions are, sometimes we just mess up, sometimes we forget, sometimes we make mistakes, and sometimes there are just accidents. We need to take a deep breath, forgive ourselves, and ask forgiveness from our children. As parents, we always hope that there is nothing too traumatic that can't be fixed. I own my mistakes and faults, but what I also try to do is learn and grow from all my experiences. I have learned that life is a lesson and once I have my ego in check, I am willing to truly live. Luckily for me, so far it has always ended up with, "It's okay, mom, I love you mom, stop being so upset, mom." But boy do I feel like shit when I mess up. Oh, *for fuck sake*, sometimes, no matter how perfect I am trying to be, I just fuck up. I've learned to take a deep breath, shrug my shoulders, and push forward.

I truly strive for normalcy. Every morning I wake up, I set my sights on having a calm, organized, peaceful day. But because they are so few and far between, sometimes it's hard for me to recognize peace and calm, as I once thought it meant. What is normal for me may not be normal for you. So, I at least try for my own normal. My plan is always the same: eat breakfast, maybe even have a cup of coffee, and begin running my errands, not rushing them – just running them. When I rush, I don't eat or drink anything until I'm overwhelmed with hunger and fatigue. Most mornings, I compromise. I won't even need to sit and eat, I'll eat on the go. I hesitate to call it a rut, yet morning reality sets in, and yet another day is upon me and reality continues to repeat itself and I find I am either skipping meals altogether or shoving food down my throat over the kitchen sink. Sound familiar? You are probably doing the same thing. Today, though, I am committed to finding a way that will be different.

It's Monday morning and it's comfortably quiet. We are starting off the week with peace. Who am I kidding? Of course, that was a fleeting moment, and as life would have it, today was an unusually crazy one. I woke up at 5:30 am with great intentions of exercising, preparing my breakfast, and taking on the day. When my husband woke up, he asked if I could give him a ride to the train station. Damn. If I take him to the station, it will ruin my chances to get in a run before the kids got up. In the past, I would have grit my teeth and drive him, forfeiting my run, and spending the rest of the day feeling resentful and defeated. This day was different, I explained to him that I woke up early specifically to exercise and was unable to take him. There. I did it, I said no. I put me first. While I felt empowered for the moment, I couldn't help feeling guilty. That's the thing with women who are managing a house with four kids and a husband. We constantly put ourselves last and then when we put ourselves first, the guilt comes creeping in to destroy our confidence. I did it though. I went for my run, came back to the house, prepped the kid's lunches, and decided to wait until later to put the yogurts in the lunch bags to keep them cold. All done with time to spare.

So far, I was winning. Lunches prepared, three loads of laundry done, replied to emails, paid the bills, and showered, and it wasn't even 7:30 yet. I was cruising. I always have more energy whenever I can get my early morning run in. Feeling good, being productive.... I made the kids breakfast, start cleaning the house, put away some dishes, I'm on top of world.... So far, this is a good Monday morning. Cruising on schedule. First, I drop off my two middle schoolers, a tad late, but still within limits to get back to the house and still have time to breathe. When I get home, I realize that William forgot his lunch. And then I realize that I forgot to put the yogurt that I purposefully left in the fridge to stay cold, to put in the other two lunch bags. *Oh, for fuck sake.*

By now, I am still finishing getting my grade schooler ready, and I'm cleaning up the teenagers' rooms. In the midst of this holy mess and the chatter going on in my head, I stay calm and find gratitude that my children (although disorganized at times) are healthy, happy, and kind people. The chatter changes to realizing that this is just a season. *Have gratitude*, I say to myself. They are happy and healthy. Anything for me not to lose my shit.

And in the middle of this, I look at the kitchen clock and think, *crap, where has the time gone?* I have to drop off all of these lunches and still get my grade schooler to school on time. And there we go. Hurry, hurry, hurry. Rush, rush, rush... drop off at the high school, drop off at the middle school, then off to the grade school for the last drop off of the day. The morning is still salvageable.

I then kiss Matthew goodbye, drive home to finish getting dressed, and I'm off to my 10:00 appointment. I did it. It all worked out. I survived another Monday morning... Until, I look over at the counter, and there it was, Williams' permission slip that is due today.

For. Fucks. Sake.

Eye roll, and a giggle. And I'm back in the car. At least I have a good sense of humor.

I could let these little mishaps ruin my day and take my joy away, but I didn't and I won't. These are all the little *for fuck sake* moments of my day, but they are never catastrophes. No one is hurt or in trouble, and life is good. Little annoyances should not define my day, or your day. If you want to change one thing today, I would suggest that you begin with training yourself to overcome the little annoyances. Keep your joy, keep your peace, and *for fuck sake,* keep your sense of humor. Was I rushed and feeling a little rattled by all the craziness this morning? Sure, I was. But what I did differently was laugh at the absurdity of all of it. If I did not have any place to be this morning, my day would have gone smoothly, guaranteed. But because I was on a time schedule, today was the day that chaos would rear its ugly head, for sure. It's life, it's real, it's aggravating and most of the time, it's fucking funny.

Chapter 9

Constant Chaos

HEY IT'S THE WEEKEND! YIPPEEEE! TGIF!

WRONG!

The thing is, when you're a parent and your kid is involved in a million different activities, Fridays signify the beginning of a very busy weekend. There's no sleeping in, no strolling shops, no cuddling on the couch, and definitely no catching a movie. Weekends are filled with running errands, sitting on ball fields, going to music classes, and schlepping kids to the mall. And when that is not on the to-do list, there are sleepovers, late-night pick-ups from parties, and constant worry. Sometimes I have fantasies of what the weekend could be, but I know that now is not the time. This is the season to raise my kids.

It used to be that each week, usually around Thursday, I would start getting excited as I thought about the possibilities for the weekend. But that was short-lived, because reality sank in, and I was once again reminded of what weekends really mean at our house. Even though by now I am used to our unplanned plans, it used to always hit me like a windstorm. I jolt back to reality and tell myself: you're not single, you have children, they need your attention, they need you. Yeah, they need me to haul their asses around all weekend long. Hey, I'm just calling it the way I see it.

When Sunday finally comes around, it's the all-day race to prepare for the coming week. Like clockwork, once Sunday evening arrives, kids across America snap out of their amnesia that plagued them all weekend. As if a silent alarm goes off, they all remember they have a report due Monday morning, they need a pair of sneakers for PE, their team jerseys need to be washed, and they are not as prepared as they should be for that major exam the next day. So, once again, I scream and yell and frantically search to find all the things they need. I try to be their hero and pull it all together by Monday morning. I know it's their responsibility, and I don't let them off the hook completely, and in the process the chatter in my head keeps asking, *for fuck sake,* why are we remembering this on Sunday night? I swear to my kids that this will never happen again, and that it's the last Sunday I'm going through this, and that I've had enough! And then the next Sunday rolls around and the same shit occurs. You are left wondering how this happened again and thinking, *for fuck sake,* I swore I'd never do this again.

The thing is, this chaos is not only reserved for Sundays before school days. It's actually a year-round way of life. On most Sunday afternoons during the summer, you can find our family on the sidelines of a kid's baseball game. We are there with all the other parents across America. If it's not some sort of ball game, it's some other kid activity. Sundays used to be reserved for family time, and now it is just more time for parents to sit for at least four hours on the sidelines of a ball game, that is generally less than what you expect. I take issue with this on so many levels. To begin with I find it unfair to my other children. It is also unfair to my family, my husband, and my family as a unit. I cannot have one child more important than the others. Having multiple children, I have learned that I need to disperse my time equally, and by having one child take over the entire family time can have a negative effect on the other kids. They might be resentful that they have to "tag" along. I have mentioned my concern to other parents and to coaches, and they seem to agree, however no one is willing to think of changes to this insane pattern. I give you my Friday nights, I give you my Saturday mornings, I give you all week with practices and games and scrimmages, but on a Sunday afternoon why can't it be that families are home together? Those traditions are almost obsolete. How can we as a society take back that time and demand that our Sundays be spent with family and friends, doing things that we want to do as a family? Whatever happened to all the family values we always speak about? How can we have family values if we don't have family time to talk about it? Everyone talks the talk, but no one is willing to walk the walk on this issue. I have to wonder if we are afraid of being bullied or black-balled by other parents who like it just the way it is. Why won't more parents admit that we don't want to be sitting on a baseball field on a sunny summer Sunday afternoon? Does that make us bad, selfish parents, or does it make us brave to want to stand up to this new age of constant movement?

I resist this because I am looking at the big picture for the well-being of the entire family and not just one member. Being at one child's game every Sunday and ignoring the other three each week is not the message I want to send to my children. Don't get me wrong, nothing makes me prouder than sitting in the stands and watching my Benjamin play baseball. I love the game more than most. I love watching my kids compete, celebrating wins and overcoming losses, but where is the balance? How can we take back our families? How can we take back our weekends? How can we take our time back? How can we not be judged for admitting that we would rather be home, than be at the baseball field corralling three other kids on a Sunday afternoon who would rather be in the comfort of their home? It just takes one voice, one seed, one thought, and that is what I am hoping to provoke.

I wonder, what happened? At what point did life force us to be so busy and hectic? When did kid sports become a business? When did little league baseball become a bigger commitment that our church, family, and weekend obligations? And *for fuck sake*, why and how did we ever allow it? Honestly, have we lost our minds? I also wonder, are the egos of the parents around me bigger than their devotion to their kids?

Being this busy does not make us better parents.

Being present does. **Read that again.**

Why is it that we would rather schlep our kids to a million activities than sit and read a book or play a board game with them? Okay, I am guilty of it as well, but my best day are those spent with my kids hanging around the house, having time to chill, and enjoying each other's company. They can unwind and be themselves and not worry about what they're wearing and how they look. A time where we are all home and relaxing. You know, we are so busy toting our kids around that we don't have time to do the small, meaningful things that we once cherished. Gone are the days of family time, dinners together, and good old free time. How healthy is this for our children, our marriage, or our families when we ignore our responsibility to help our children grow stress free and with a creative imagination and an insatiable curiosity? What about you? Do you have family down time?

During the summer my son, Benjamin, was traveling with his baseball team. After spending all spring and now most of the summer keeping up with his games, my daughter finally spoke up. "Why are you never home? I can't do anything because of Benjamin's baseball!" And she was right. Benjamin became more important that the rest of the kids because his extracurricular activity was absorbing all of our time, affecting everyone. There must be a balance. Some sort of compromise.

I suppose you are thinking that there is nothing we can do, it's just the way it is, and we can't change it now. To that, I say bullshit! Take back your family. Hold on to your morals. You may not win every battle, and of course there will be sacrifices to make, but my kids know family is going to come first and I'm not going to be sorry. Now, I'm not talking about high school because there is a certain responsibility that comes with being on a varsity team. I'm talking about grade school. Have you noticed that over the past ten years, the age keeps getting younger for competitive sports, and the demands keep getting higher? These kids don't have the maturity or the attention span for such a vigorous schedule. Some parents may challenge me with that statement and respond with, "Well, then don't sign them up for sports at all!" But my feeling is, there's got to be a balance. Why can't our young children play a sport without it being a 6-day-a-week commitment? Actually, I know the answer to this one. Here it comes: EGO. I spend a lot of time on the sidelines where I see kids walking off the field crying, climbing the fence, kicking the dirt in complete boredom, running around causing havoc, while parents are in a constant state of scream. Yelling for their kids playing in the game and yelling at their other kids who are bored out of their minds. Sometimes parents don't say nice things to their "star" player. "Run, jump, kick, pay attention, wake up, what are you looking at?" It makes my skin crawl to watch them behave like this. It breaks my heart to watch a kid's spirits deflate because of the public scolding they are getting from their parents to DO BETTER! Now, if that's not EGO talking, I don't know what is. Are you okay that your kids hear your angry disapproving voice and internalize it as disappointment from you and not enthusiasm?

On the other hand, my kids know full well that when they are on the field, certain behaviors will not be tolerated. The expectations are clear in my house, if you are on the field you are representing yourself, your family, and your team. You are to have good sportsmanship, listen to the coaches, and do your best. The moment when we don't see the effort, is the day your sports career ends. To this day, we have never had an issue with any of this because the guidelines have already been clearly communicated, just as they know we will never embarrass them with bad behavior from the sidelines. Parenting is a give and take. It is a balance of what we feel and what we say. We have allowed the chaos around us to modify our behavior. Is the theory the louder you yell from the sidelines, the more involved you will seem? Here's the truth, it's all just noise. Get out of what you think society wants you to be and get back to being a supportive parent that is just happy to sit and watch your kid do what he or she loves to do!

I believe that there is a correlation between what I call "constant movement" and the impact it has had on our generation of millennials. They are viewed as needy and selfish, indulgent and lazy. But who is raising this so-called "self- righteous" generation? We are. As parents we must take some responsibility for what we are seeing. They are raised to be more important, more time consuming. and more valued than the generations in the past. It is true, every generation blames the past generation, but in the 21st century, we need to find ways to raise happy, content people who understand that the world does not revolve around them. While I know many of the challenges that the millennial generation are up against, they also have so many incredible qualities. They are innovative, they enjoy life, they are more compassionate and aware of the world than my generation has ever been. They are more sensitive and, in some cases, they are far kinder. They've been taught not to bully, not to belittle, and to treat people of equal value. In my experience as a child, we made fun of people all the time. From their ethnic background to the clothes they were wearing, nothing was off limits and it was just part of growing up. No one used the word bully. And if they did, it was for good reason. I think the word bully has been taken out of context in some cases. Sometimes kids are just poking fun at one another and it's not bullying. Obviously if it is constant and consistent that is a totally different situation than what I'm referring to. The lines get blurry sometimes on this matter, but kindness is important and I'm all for more of that.

Sometimes we all get into a pity party. We do not intend to have the pity party, we did not intend to stay at the pity party, but there we are: in our own personal pity party. During these times, there will be people who will attend your pity party and then there are people who will drop by your pity party, tell you it was fun, and tell you when it's over. Those are the best people. I'm not one to have many pity parties, but it does happen, it's a part of life. I am a strong-willed woman and when I find my children having their own pity party, I'm the one to tell them, "Okay, time to get back up, wipe yourself off, and move forward." Hearing this from their mother is far better than getting their feelings hurt by someone who doesn't really know the ins and outs of who they are. So often, I hear them say, "It's not fair, it wasn't my fault." I gently remind them that while it's okay to feel sorry for a little while, they must also figure out a way to move forward, move on, and try again. It breaks my heart when my kids aren't invited to a sleep-over, didn't get a part in the play, didn't make the team, or wasn't invited to hang out with friends. I understand their sadness, I talk it out with them. I even try to play devil's advocate to get them to see the other side of the situation, but inevitably – when we are all talked out, I tell them to move on. Being angry, being sad, and being a victim at your own pity party will do nothing but self-destruct. My advice? Feel it, own it, and then *for fuck sake,* move on.

Being busy is a relative term. For you, busy might mean having a tight schedule or missing a work deadline or carting kids around to their next activity. It seems we work more hours, the schools demand more of our time, our children demand more of our attention, sports and other activities demand a strong commitment, more than ever before. I wonder, is this really good for our kids? Or is it good for us, in some sort of ego-maniacal way? My mom once observed, "You parent's today make up shit for yourselves to do." She's right. I don't remember a time when my parents were at every meeting at the school, when there were meetings about school field trips, and that sports and other activities filled their lives with appointments, deadlines, and driving all over town. I cannot recall a time on a Sunday afternoon that my parents were on the sidelines of a field instead of in their home.

One last word about this. I have four children, one child is into sports; therefore, I find myself leaving the other three at home while I attend to that one child's sports game. My other three children are basically home doing whatever they can to fend for themselves - almost 5 days a week. Usually, I don't walk through the door until almost 8:00 pm, after having sat on the sidelines for the past 3 hours, because of sports. Now, let me clarify. I am not anti-kids sports; I am pro- what the hell is going on in my house when I'm at the game. My kids get home from school around 3:30, so that doesn't leave much time to square away the plan for while I'm gone, especially when there's homework to complete and dinner to make. I've often asked my husband, are the rewards worth the effort? Are we making one child more important than the other three? When I think about the hours each week that my kids spend home alone without their dad or me, I question whether this is good for my family. I don't think that this is good for our society. I believe that less is more. Most parents (me included) are caught in the web of running around, making deadlines, chauffeuring kids, making it to school meetings, and keeping up with what it takes to have a healthy and happy family. I would love to be able to take back our families, take back our weekends, and take back our Sunday afternoons. I think if enough people feel the same way we can make a grassroots effort to be part of the **less is more** movement that provides less stressful and much happier families across America.

Chapter 10

A Piece of Peace

LESS IS MORE, AND MORE IS JUST CHAOTIC AND UNNECESSARY, unless we are talking about cake. What is with the more, more, more mentality? More practices, more games, more activities, more get-togethers, more obligations. In a nutshell: more unnecessary bullshit! There. I said it.

I was speaking to a mother of two young children who are each in four different activities. They are carted from one activity to the next during the week and on weekends. That's 2 children times 4 activities each, to equal 8 activities on 7 days a week. When they finally arrive home, a timer is set to eat dinner within ten minutes, and then it's reading time, then off to bed. No play time, no down time, no family time, just go, go, go; then come home and do it again. And these are grade school children.

One day, a woman started up a conversation with me. She was incredibly frazzled. I know the look. She talked about how her four-year-old is in four different activities each day. Time for math again. That's 1 child, times 4 activities a day, times (possibly) 7 days a week, to equal 28 activities per week. Is it just me, or is that too much of an overload? Can our children's teeny bodies handle the physical and mental demands of being in so many activities? When do they get to play for play's sake? There has to be a balance.

We must realize that we are programming our children to be high stress and always "on." Believe it or not, kids need alone time. They need time to process, and wonder. They need time to grow through their childhood without stress or worry. Sometimes parents get caught up with treating their children like adults by giving them rigid schedules and signing them up for high-demanding activities. What are we gaining? Why do our children have to be involved in so many organized activities now? What happened to playing outside and using their imagination without it being scheduled?

I think about this concept of activity-overload every day. It baffles me. I often ask parents why their children are involved in so many activities and here are their answers: it keeps them busy, I don't want them sitting around the house driving me crazy, it's good for their character, they don't mind going. Oh, *for fuck sake,* whatever happened to just playing? I will tell you the truth, and you may not like it. Are you ready? We may have to actually step it up as parents and be more attentive to our children if we all stayed home. Parenting is challenging and it is up to us to develop routines, expectations, family time, and getting along as a team. With four kids, we are a constant activity as a unit. I am in the middle of it with them along the way. It works for us. Honestly, at this moment, I am regrettably overscheduled. Playing baseball or soccer or basketball no longer means a game or two a week. It is now a lifestyle commitment. It's practice three times a week, two games a week, tournaments and scrimmages on holiday weekends. It's now a seven-day-a-week-commitment. It's way beyond a habit or hobby, it's a regiment. *For fuck sake*, when did their extracurricular activities breach our family and take over our lives?

Now, I am an active person who likes to keep busy, but there has to be some sort of balance. Look around you. It should be obvious. As a society, we are lacking balance. We are expected to do and produce and be so much more than ever before. I am not convinced it is good for our children, ourselves, or our society.

I have a plan to take back our family time. I propose to stop being pressured into over- scheduling, because I have learned that it affects every member of our family. We are in a constant state of unnecessary busy. You know, everyone says time moves too fast, but it is really just a state of mind. You are affected by how you spend each moment of your life. I propose that we be present, instead of always pushing and planning for the future; everything from tonight's dinner to tomorrow afternoon's baseball game. Isn't is reasonable to want to be present? You deserve the time and energy to embrace all these moments instead of racing through them because there are ten other things still to do for that day. I remind myself of this daily because I am guiltier than most about this. One lesson I'm learning more than any other, is that I can't say yes to everything. I can't be everything to everyone, all of the time, and sometimes shit happens and I'm going to be a couple of minutes late and you know what, it will all be okay, **because I would rather be present with my kids than perfect with the world.** (*another AHA moment*)

There is no point in getting uptight. It does no one any good. Everything I do and every plan I make happens with my children in mind. I pride myself on being on time almost all of the time, which usually makes everyone frantic and stressed. Sometimes, being a couple of minutes late so that my kid can finish up a homework assignment is going to have to be all right. I have spent years of striving for perfection and failing miserably, and so now I know that it is okay to be perfectly imperfect. We have come so far and we are doing all right, so I know it's actually a healthier reality. We are a busy family and we all try to work as a team.

I have finally embraced the fact that I am perfectly imperfect, and now I wear it like a badge of honor. Perfection is no longer viewed as a virtue and imperfection is no longer one of my downfalls. I no longer apologize for it, nor look for the perfection I once sought. I am just me. Perfectly imperfect me. I learned this from my children and I am grateful for their input. And that is how I find my piece of peace. How do you find yours?

Is it completely unrealistic and unattainable? Or is it just something to strive for each day? Take a look around. By becoming more aware of the chaos around us, you will notice how everyone is reacting to their own personal stress. You know what I mean. The rude guy on line at the Stop and Shop. The woman in the truck who gave you the finger. Your boss, your co-worker, your... your... well, you know who those people are. That's a lot of outside negative energy coming straight at you. It makes your mind race, your insides shake, and your determination stronger in getting everything to work. Despite what you might be up against, you can always find a way to compete with the constant fast pace of life.

Is that how we want to live? If the answer is no, what can we do to change it?

First, it is time to examine your family routines. Our children still live a busy life with school work, sports, and extracurricular activities. They also have church friendships that get together once a week. So, what exactly can we do to make our lives more peaceful? It is simple. Slow down. Take your time to enjoy the small glorious moments of each day. Even within all the chaos and all the craziness, take a moment to acknowledge it, accept it, and do so in the moment. That's what it means to be present. Really, really present. It's harder to do than you think. I know this because I am guilty, too. When I am out with my kids, my self-talk is constantly reminding me to stop checking social media, stop scrolling through emails, and stop listening to voicemails on speaker phone.

Watch the game, enjoy the time, seize the moment. Make the stuff you are doing enjoyable, instead of spending your time, planning for the next activity that pulls you away from being home with your family. Then learn to say no. We all struggle with this one. We don't need to be on every committee, participate in every activity, attend every meeting, and go to every single party. There are times we can just say no. Of course, we don't want to disappoint people, so we wrap ourselves up in so much chaos, by continually saying yes, when we really want to say no. This is absurd. Think about all the energy you are putting into dealing with all the other adults, and stressing about not disappointing anyone, and all of a sudden, you are all in. I mean swallowed in. Do you see where I am going with this? There are things that can be arranged and done at home that could build the same traits that being in activities could offer. When you think of your family as a team, and your family has the ability to work together, you work together. What you learn; what I have learned, is that good is good enough. In fact, it's perfectly good enough.

We don't have to be perfect. We don't have to look perfect, have a perfect home, drive the perfect car, go on the perfect vacation, or have the perfect children. Constant perfection will drive us nuts! Unnecessary stress and unnecessary worry will unnecessarily bring chaos into our lives. Frankly, I am a bit of a neat freak. I like my home in order, I like the laundry done, and I like everything just so, but I'm trying to allow myself to let some of that go. For me living in a clean environment is an absolute must, I'm non-negotiable about that. There were times where I wouldn't even sit down if there was something out of place. Today, I can proudly say, I have learned that somethings can wait. And sometimes, *for fuck sake*, I just close the kids' bedroom doors and walk away.

Having integrity with your intention to be present, and to allow imperfections, and to slow down will bring a piece of peace to your life. By being flexible and willing to change the way you do things in order to achieve these things will help with your success for peace. Embrace these changes, so you can embrace the moments, the real moments. You know, the moments that really matter. Nothing lasts forever, so all of this *for fuck sake* craziness that we experience every day will not last forever, for this is just a season. One day I know that I will look around my home and there will be no laundry to fold, no toys to pick up, no dishes to put away, or any whiffle balls to collect from the front lawn. And I will miss it. But the love and the laughter and the life that I have built with my family will never, ever be taken away.

My hope is that you take advantage of these years and understand enough to embrace the fact that that this will not last forever. Despite all the *fucks sake*, stress, worry, and complete and utter chaos, there is so much joy, and an abundance of gratitude. Grateful, that I get to be the mom of these perfectly imperfect children, gratitude that I get to have a supportive, kind and loving husband, gratitude that I am surrounded by real friends who are honest, loving and true to me, gratitude that I have siblings, along with their spouses, who are also my friends, and nieces and nephews that I get to see grow and be part of their lives. Yes, there is an abundance of gratitude, and an overwhelming feeling of love.

Chapter 11

The Sisterhood of Motherhood

YEARS AGO, I WAS IN MEXICO AT ONE OF THOSE FANCY ALL-IN-clusive resorts. This particular day was spent at the beach. The weather was beautiful, the sand was soft, and I was enjoying my time in the clear blue water. My oldest son, William, was swimming with a bunch of boys that he had just met, none of which spoke English. As I watched them swim and play together, within a blink of an eye, I noticed that a riptide started taking the boys out farther into the ocean. My first obvious instinct was to save my own son. Once I got him safely to shore, I noticed that one of the larger boys started going under. I watched his head slip down into the water three times. I was terrified, but my mother instinct kicked in immediately. I swam out to the boy and struggled to get him to safety. He was heavy, and tired, and he was scared. By then, many people on the beach started to notice the commotion in the water and started to run toward me. As I was gasping for my own breath I just kept saying, "It's going to be okay." In what seemed like forever, I finally got this boy to dry land. Standing there in a complete state of panic was his mother telling me something in Spanish as tears flowed down her face. She was looking at me and holding her son saying, "Gracías." She looked into my eyes and I into hers, and for a quick moment we exchanged a deep soulful connection. She didn't have to speak the same language for me to understand her gratitude. At the end of the day, mothers help mothers, with no judgment, and I was just happy to have saved this little boy from drowning.

Far too often, mothers judge each other for the wrong reasons. Instead, the sisterhood of motherhood should be an important "safety net" for all women. We should be there to help one another without judgment. Too often, women's egos get in the way of the true meaning of motherhood. Sometimes to make ourselves feel better, we somehow think that we have to make others feel worse for their shortcomings. I remember one time I forgot to give one of my children money for the school book fair. I'm pretty on target with these things, but I simply just forgot. There were other mothers there that could have saved my child from embarrassment and given him a couple of dollars, knowing full well that I would repay them. After all, I knew these mothers, and they knew my child. Instead, my son sat in the corner and could not purchase a book. *For fuck sake,* help a sister out. Mother to mother, I ask you – put yourselves in the shoes of kid without book money and everyone else is buying books. Now, I know plenty of mothers who would have given my son a couple of dollars and never even mentioned it to me. However, on this particular day, there was not one mother there that was willing to do so. In fact, when these mothers saw me, the first words out of their mouths were, "What's the matter with you, you forgot to give your kid money for the book fair!"

C'mon now, we are on the same team. It's not about one-upmanship, nor is it about how great you are or how great I am. It's about helping, whether we know each other or not. To all the moms: We are in this together! *For fuck sake*, if you see a mother who dropped the ball on something, catch it. That's what the sisterhood of motherhood is all about. That experience taught me that whenever I see another mother's child needing a couple of bucks for the book fair, or any other fair, *for fuck's sake,* I will hand him or her some money. I will be taking the high road without making his mother feel like shit.

Sisterhood of motherhood. For the most part, mothers I know go above and beyond to share rides, copy homework or remind other mothers about the book fair, the student store, or if there are special events happening at school. We have a wonderful network for our kids' activities, and for that I am so grateful. For my sake, we have a strong sisterhood of motherhood in this community. *Rock on, Sisters of the Motherhood!*

Trying to balance motherhood with my daily commitments of work, marriage, running a household, having friends, and volunteering in my community while still having some sort of peace of mind is always a challenge. This balance comes from things I know about, and there's a whole set of balancing acts in place for the unexpected.

Some people say that multitasking doesn't work. Well, I would bet every woman who is in the sisterhood of motherhood knows that multitasking really **does** work well. Women multitask at a rate like never before. The difference between our generation and the generation before us is that we are demanding more me-time. I don't remember my mother really having (or wanting me-time), unless to her, it was sitting on her favorite chair watching *All My Children* every single day of my childhood, from what I can remember. I am sure she had her own struggles and challenges raising her children, and perhaps, though it wasn't spoken about the way it is today, she didn't know what it meant to have true alone time where she could reflect and appreciate herself and her family.

I hate to say this, but I find that many women today are more apt to compare my life, my children, my marriage, my home, and my vacations to their own. I used to feel embarrassed that I did not work outside my house. I felt I was being judged, which made me defensive. Like I had to prove to someone else that because I did not work outside my home, it did not diminish my worth in society. Admittedly, I was not someone who had to answer to a boss, or have work deadlines, or worry about salary, or status, or even promotions.

I soon realized that no one can make me feel anything without my permission. (This is another of those lines where I think you should read it again). No one can make me feel anything without my permission. I call it "being in my head and not paying rent." I've got to kick it out of my mind. So, I stopped explaining myself, and that made all the difference in the world. Truly, I can admit that it was life changing. I no longer feel the guilt or embarrassment because I know I am doing what is right for my own family, just as they are doing what's right for theirs. It's not a competition, it's living our own truths. These are words that I embrace.

Deciding to stay home with my children was an easy choice. I had a great job, made good money, and was good at it, but I knew when I had children all of that would change. I gave up my career, gave up the extra money, and lived on a very tight budget to be home with my children. It was not always easy financially, emotionally, or mentally. It was just something I knew that was right for my family. As is turned out, after having four children (born two years apart) I researched full time childcare costs if I were to consider returning to work. As you can imagine, with four kids, financially, it was not doable. When we considered our kids would have two full time working parents away from the house (and them) at least 8-10 hours a day, we knew it wasn't for us. Not only is it expensive to get someone to watch them, it leaves about four or five hours to come together with the family; or do laundry, or check homework, or make lunches for the next day, or iron a blouse or two, or…. well, again, you can see where this is going. Time away from my children, beyond being unsettling in itself, was just not worth the extra money I would be contributing to our family.

Now, this may be hard for you to accept, but here is comes anyway. We don't need more money; what we need is more time with our children – building our family team, playing games, and helping them grow, and having movie night, and big breakfasts on Sundays, and no one is exhausted and crabby because two working parents don't have much time for family fun! And then my decision was clear. Having my college degree in hand, and the potential in my head get a high-paying job to make a lot of money to buy a lot of things, I looked around at my family and knew that I had all the things I needed. I knew I wanted to stay home with my children. In the beginning when they were younger, I was on autopilot. I was incredibly busy and wasn't thinking about what the mothers around me were doing or the money I wasn't making.

I was spending my days caring for my children and my home and making family memories with my husband and our one, two, three, then four kids. I was happy to make sure that all their needs were met, and there were times just trying to keep it all together was the goal of the day. But even in that moment, if you would have asked me if I regretted my decision, I would tell you not in the least. Yet, as the children got older and started school, other parents made remarks about my lack of employment.

I have always been a driven woman, and everyone who knew me, knew that my ability to focus positive energy in a certain positive direction is uncanny. There was a time that I felt very insecure, and those insecurities took me on a journey down the horrible road of self-doubt. Throughout my life, I find I have to prove things to myself to verify the truth. So, I jumped in. I became involved in everything in the school, as well as earn certifications in nutrition and fitness. All the pieces were sort of coming together, and I started my own business as a health coach. Once I jumped in, I also became a running coach, the Vice President of the Kiwanis's club, was on the church board, and then… Wait for it. I was running ragged.

At first, I loved the excitement. I felt important for the first time outside of my home, in a long time. Don't get me wrong, feeling important at home makes me feel like a million bucks. But it's my family. We like each other. My work was satisfying and I enjoyed the accolades, earning my own money and the excellent feeling of self-worth. This went on for a couple of years and as time wore on, I became distant from my family and more and more involved in other people's lives and their best interests, rather than the interests of the people under my roof. You know, money and power are a weird combination and should not interrupt a family of six. My marriage was failing, my kids were miserable, and deep down inside I felt a tremendous amount of guilt for not being truly the person I really wanted to be. It was around that time that I started to notice my children's personalities changing. They were becoming less patient, less kind, and more reclusive. The communication in my relationship with my husband broke down, and we struggled to figure out our "new norm." I was driven to make a name for myself, but when I looked really hard, I realized that the name I was making was not the name I wanted to be. It became clear one night when I was at yet another Kiwanis Club dinner meeting. I knew my kids were home that night, and Emma had an important project due the next day.

The speaker talked about our mission of saving children around the world. Ironically, sitting there listening, taking in his words and his message, it hit me like a ton of bricks. An overwhelming feeling of clarity came over me. There I was, sitting at a meeting about saving children around the world when my own children were at home with a babysitter. What the hell was I doing there? And *for fuck sake*, why the hell wasn't I home?

My life at that moment stopped. I realized my true meaning of self was dismantling, and that I was off course to my integral mission and plan for my family. I felt like I betrayed my children and I resented all the choices I made to push myself to be successful. Only to prove to myself that I could do it and to others that I was a worthy working mom. In doing so, I lost sight of the mom I used to be. I immediately began the process of pulling back, and soon learned that being "important" to people outside of my home is not near as satisfying as being important to my children in our home. I resigned from the Kiwanis club, stepped down as a board member of the church, and slowly disassembled my business.

Creating and running a business was on my bucket list, and now I can check it off. I know where my priorities are. I guess I just had something to prove. Okay. Been there. Done that. But not without learning some valuable lessons. I also learned that to me, my family is everything.

Since that defining moment, I began shifting priorities and putting all of the "out of the house" energy into "in the house" energy. I organized family time, reading time, game nights, movie nights and sleepovers. I promoted the Morandi name by teaching my kids our traditions and habits and how we all stand for kindness and staying positive. We worked and played and learned together all under one roof. We planned and cooked and delegated chores and our family ran like a clock. (Well, one that somehow always made the kids late!) I took all of my "outside" energy and poured it into my family. I guess I had to experience the consequences of my decision to push – gung-ho – toward building my outside persona in order to realize that what really mattered was what was going on at home.

The point is, I realized that I was not living my truth. My personal truth. One of my most favorite quotes is from Maya Angelou: "When you know better, you do better." I find that when I get caught up with all the noise of society, I allow my parenting to be consumed by expectations. But once I realize that I am not in balance with MY truth I quickly readjust my intentions because once I know better, I do better. When your integrity and intent is intact, and you are living your own truth there is nothing that can stop you. I continue to keep these truths in mind while raising children. How about you? Are you real with whatever your truth may be? It's not as easy as it sounds. My hope is that you will be able to do that because when you know better, you do better.

My lesson is to live my own truth, to be real with myself. We all need to find the balance between ourselves and our family. How do you make it work? And do you have harmony? Don't listen to the voices outside, don't let that noise get into your head because it may lead to regret. Be you. If that is a working mom or if that is a stay at home mom or if that is anything in between, be you. One thing I have learned is that your children will love you anyway.

When I was in the thick of building up my business, I spent many hours beating myself up for not being good enough. I kept pushing for perfection. When I finally released that burden, it brought me positive energy and incredibly, my life changed. I no longer let others' opinions get in the way of my own journey. It doesn't matter if I'm working or not, if I'm a laid-back parent or a strict parent, or if I hang out in sweats and a tee shirt all day long. None of that really matters, as long as I am being true. I see how the root of most issues facing us today is based on listening to all the outside noise.

In the name of living your truth, I propose for you to release the noise! Don't care so much about what others may perceive as your truth, and do not to compare your journeys to others because you own your journey. If everyone would take a step back and consider this, the deafening noise will become a quieter roar.

Stay on your own path, leave your own legacy, and *for fuck sake* stop worrying about everything else! If you free yourself from all of the outside noise around you, you can bet that your life, your children's lives, your family, and your well-being will be so much more at peace.

Chapter 12

Pull Yourself Together

At some point early on when I was having and raising children, I got into fitness. I started running races, then marathons, then triathlons and eventually completed a half Ironman. I love running because I am able to filter my emotions. The art of running is one of the most treasured activities that I perform. Someone once asked me why I run 30 to 50 miles per week. It was common to hear that corny joke, "Hey, Donna! What are you running from?" That is an interesting question, but it does bring up a point. Why do I run? Do I do it for my health? Do I do it to keep fit? Do I do it to clear my mind? Do I do it just because I like it? Do I do it to run away from the house? Well, actually, yes. All of these.

Reality is, avid runners run for that feeling of a nice long run. They love the runner's high, the invigorating adrenaline, and that combination feeling of invigoration and calm when it's over. Words cannot really do it justice. Regardless, the question was valid. Was I running to run away? The challenges of being a mother and demanding perfection is exhausting. I spend much of my days cleaning and tidying and organizing that I am completely exhausted - running makes me feel free. A run is where no one can catch me or ask me for something. A run is just me, the pavement, and my own thoughts. My heavy breath, strong body, determined mind always remind me of the power I have within. So, to answer that question, I'm not running away as much as I'm running to remind myself of who I am. Running is my Zen place, and everyone benefits when mommy has her run.

With the laundry overflowing, the chaos at the house, the bills needing to be paid, and dinner needing to be cooked, I find myself relying on my daily run to get my thoughts in order. When I'm at home, I cannot control anyone's mood, homework load, or how the night will play out. When I run I'm in control, I get to decide how far, how fast, and what music I will be listening to during my run. It gives me a sense of going somewhere and coming back. I feel empowered when I run because I spend my time feeling every second of everything happening, and along the way, I can sort out my next move when I return home to the kids.

I am running to remind myself who I am, what I could accomplish, and that my mind and body is strong. As my legs burn in pain, and I feel the sweat dripping down my face, my heart rate is pumping, while my lungs are inhaling every last inch of breath, I feel on top of the world. Running makes me a better mother, wife, friend, and family member because it fills my soul with joy and releases all the day's tensions. Running reminds me that I'm human, I'm a woman, and I am my own person. Running reminds me that although I am so many things to so many people, I have hopes, fears and feelings of my own. While running, I have an outlet to work through all of these emotions so that I can better police my behavior when I return home to my children. I feel powerful, strong, confident and in control when I run. I cannot control everything that happens to my children or my family. I cannot make my children feel confident, that is something they need to learn on their own. Although I can build them up emotionally as much as possible, I cannot force them to be strong in all situations. Running has given me the tools to be both emotionally, physically, and mentally strong. I hope that my children will find a healthy outlet as well. I remember when I first started running I was happy, but I felt like nothing was mine. And the mere hour a day, which technically is just 5% of my day, was dedicated to me – my time – and it was invigorating. While running, the children certainly couldn't catch me, and it was a place, actually the only place, where I could be alone. It was my solace and still is. In fact, now I run with a couple of very close friends of mine, and although I'm not alone per se, I get to enjoy a friendship and the camaraderie of women who enjoy the same activity, respect each other, and have strong affections for one another. Certainly, running could be replaced with Zumba, yoga, basketball, golf, tennis, or even hiking, as well as many non-physical activities. But for me, running is my escape, my love, and the part of me that I hope I will get to enjoy for the rest of my life.

One distinct triathlon stands out from the rest. I was in the water during the swim part of the race and just at the most inopportune time, I experienced my first ever panic attack. Having a panic attack is hard enough, but during a triathlon in freezing cold water exaggerated the event even more. I felt paralyzed, I didn't know what to do. There I was, flaming out both mentally and physically in the middle of the bay with hundreds of spectators everywhere. I was mortified and horrified. I tried to get my head together, but I found it difficult to function. I tried to take a breath. I tried to stay focused. No matter what I did, anxiety kept building for what seemed like an eternity. I finally got out of the water and continued on with the race. I was rattled to my core, but knew I had to go on. The next event of the race was biking. My knees were weak, I was dizzy, and my adrenaline was pumping at an unbelievable and probably dangerous rate. Halfway through the bike event I started to pull myself together. By the time I was switching out of my bike shoes and into my sneakers for the run part of the event, I was finally completely back in control.

In the end, I fared well in the race but was shaken by my own anxiety and how it made me feel. I learned an important lesson that day: no matter what is happening, no matter how scared and fearful I may be, I must continue to go on. I will not let that fear overcome my goals. In retrospect, I did more than just finish the race, I persevered despite the chaos in my head that was trying to mess with my courage. After that, I continued doing triathlons and eventually completed a half Ironman. I could have just finished that one triathlon and felt proud that I did it and be done with it. But that wasn't going to be good enough for me. I didn't let that one experience stop me from ever doing it again. Believe me, while I was in the water, I thought about quitting, I mumbled more than once, *for fuck sake*, but I continued. I kept on going, despite how I was feeling at the peak of my anxiety. Had I quit that first triathlon, I would have never continued my journey in the fitness world. I would have never achieved my goals. I would have let fear decide my destiny. And more importantly, I know I would have regretted it.

I wonder, do you have regrets? Have you ever found yourself frozen with fear and didn't know what to do? Even when you feel like you may be drowning, and you are paralyzed with tremendous fear and anxiety, and you don't know what you're going to do or how are you going to get out of a situation, your only choice is to pull yourself together and keep going. This is a lesson that I remind my children of often. They need to truly understand it so they don't find themselves isolated in their own thoughts, wallowing in their own pity. For every failure, there is a greater lesson. You just have to be open to find it.

The last time I ran in the New York City Marathon was in 2015. I had a goal in mind, and that was to do my personal best and finish the race in four hours. I was determined, I was well-trained, and I was ready. The crowds in New York were incredible that day, the energy alone can have you running for miles and miles without even realizing it. As I passed each mile marker, I did so with very little effort. I was in the zone and on target to meet my expectations. Unfortunately, I did not account for my very sensitive stomach. I got a stomach cramp, and at first the pain with slight, but it became increasingly more uncomfortable as each mile passed. I was determined to persevere, finish the race with a time I could be proud of. However, by the time I reached mile 20, my pace had slowed down, but I was still powering forward and still determined to finish. When I reached mile 26, I was almost certain that I would not make my expected time of four hours. Instead of giving up, I was more determined than ever to finish the race strong, confident, and proud. I knew I would have to look my friends, family, and children in the eye and be accountable for my effort. Although the reality of me not finishing in the time I had hoped for was very real in my mind and in my spirit, I finished that race with a big smile and a bigger sense of accomplishment at four hours, one minute, and eight seconds. If you're a runner you know that the first thought in my head as I crossed the finish line was, *oh for fuck sake*, I missed it by 68 seconds. Luckily, for non-runners that time doesn't even matter. My kids congratulated me, my family high fived me, and no one even asked what my time was. Only thing was, I knew that I did not reach it, and I was a little disappointed. On the flip side, I was proud because even when I realized I wouldn't reach the time I was going for, my speed did not decrease. In fact, it increased at the end. I did not give up, I kept persevering and ran as fast as I could to that finish line, to finish strong and be true to myself.

To this day, I still use the example of the New York City Marathon when I talk to my children about reaching their goals. I remind them that they are not always going to succeed the first time, but no matter what, don't ever give up. When things seem impossible, you push harder, finish strong, and always be proud. It was like that for me as a child who couldn't read, and it was still the case with this marathon. To date, I have yet to reach my goal of the four-hour mark, but I keep that lesson it taught me close to my heart and hope to achieve that goal one day. We shall see.

Chapter 13

Just when you think...

I THINK MY PERSPECTIVE OF MOTHERHOOD AND LIFE CAN bring value to others. It is an honest account of how we all go through so many situations in our own lives, and that with a little sense of humor, it can be a series of entertaining life lessons. Sometimes you just need to search for them a little harder, but most times, the lessons are there.

No matter how much you love your children, they're going to do things that will hurt your feelings. When you are doing your best to be a good parent, compassionate listener, being fully present, and providing solid guidance, you will still be unappreciated. It's a hard truth.

One day my pre-teen daughter was at the movies and no one else had arrived yet. While she was waiting for her friend, I decided to wait with her because I felt uncomfortable leaving her at a movie theater alone. I sat far away from her and waited for her friends to arrive. When they got there, I simply walked up to her and asked if she was all set or if she needed me to buy the tickets, get the snacks, or wait to make sure that she was able to get into the theater. I thought that I was being helpful; she on the other hand did not. Unknowingly, I embarrassed her in front of all of her friends. She shot back, "Shoo fly, Shoo, go fly away, just go." I was hurt, embarrassed and angry. It was one of those *for fuck sake* moments, that left me pondering, how could my precious beautiful child speak to me so cruelly when I was only there to help? I learned from that moment, that while I was trying to make sure my child was safe and happy, I was also being overbearing and embarrassing in a pre-teen's eyes. I was stunned and hurt, but I didn't react immediately. Later, I was relieved to learn that she felt awful about the way she treated me. After the movie and her friends went their separate ways and we were alone, my daughter immediately apologized and asked for my forgiveness. Although her behavior was unacceptable and there were consequences to follow, it made me happy to know that she took responsibility for her actions, apologized, and was willing to make things right. When your children mess up and learn from it, that is what makes something negative become a positive life lesson. You have to take what you can get from an experience, and even with hurt feelings, move on.

It is a good thing that I am not easily offended. Sitting at the kitchen table, William jokingly announces, "Mom, I like Dad more," and then the other three kids agreed.

"Why?" I was baffled.

"Well because he buys all the things around here, he's a role model because he is successful, so we just like him better."

I stood there in utter disbelief, thinking *for fuck sake*, I have given up my job, a career, so much of myself, all of my wants and desires to be here to take care of all of you full-time. Yeah, I was hurt, but I was also amused by his words. How could they like Peter more than me? After my shock wore off, I thought more rationally. Their dad never says no, he buys them pretty much anything they want, he doesn't have to deal with curfews or homework or grades or discipline. He just gets to be there and be their dad. When I look at it that way, I would like him better, too! Peter is interesting, fun, rarely says no, and is always willing to go above and beyond, and all our kids know it.

With their new proclamation of admiration for their father, I thought back to their baby and toddler years where all they ever wanted was mommy, mommy, mommy. I know Peter felt a slight bit of jealousy during those years, and I felt a great sense of accomplishment that all my sacrifice paid off because they always only wanted me. Now the tides have turned. They are older, they are more independent, they find him more interesting, smarter and more exciting. At first, I was hurt and a little insulted, but then realized - who wouldn't like him more? He is all the things they imagine him to be, and I'm happy that out of all the people in the world I found a person who is wonderful, kind, and generous to our children. Their father shows them how great life can be, and by example, proves to them how the benefits of hard work and dedication can produce a fulfilling life. I hope all of them strive to be like their father: hard-working, dedicated, smart, fun, and exciting, I also know that from my influence, I am raising kind, compass loving, and caring people to complement their father's attributes.

Every day, one of my kids jolt me back to reality. I find it comforting to know that they can poke fun at me and it will end in a hardy laugh and me acting even more ridiculous. If I took every time my daughter, Emma, made a disparaging comment about my face, my hair or my outfit, I would never leave the house. I would also be ready for a facelift, a new wardrobe, and a whole bunch of therapy sessions. I take it with a grain of salt. I like to think that they're saying it in a loving, fun way. I'm not so sure that's true, but that's at least what I'm going to make myself believe. The other day I was going for the relaxed weekend grunge look. I had a new outfit on: cargo pants, a striped shirt, and a flannel over it. I thought I looked pretty cool, I had seen some of the celebrities wear this kind of outfit. However, when I went to say good night to my son, William, he looked up from his phone, and said "I see you're doing the lesbian look today." My reaction? I busted out laughing because that morning when I looked in the mirror my first thought was William is going to make fun of me, and my second thought was I don't really care.

Another time, I had just come home from getting my hair dyed and cut and was feeling quite pretty that day. I was dressed in one of my favorite sundresses, my hair was shiny, and I was even wearing some make up. Benjamin took one look at me and without any hesitation said, "Oh, I see you dyed your hair again and are trying to look young. It's not gonna happen, Mom… your time has passed." I didn't know whether to laugh, cry, reprimand him, or crawl inside a hole. Of course, I laughed hysterically and thought, *oh, for fuck sake*, he's right. Just when I think I look good and feel good about how I look, one of my kids will take me down a few notches. Kids have a way of putting you in your place and keeping life in perspective. Once, when I was watching the American Music Awards, my man crush, Justin Timberlake, came on stage. I was admiring him with all his talent, looks, and swag to my son, Benjamin. As I was gushing about my admiration for this worldwide singing icon, my then five-year old, asked, "Who's that?" Jokingly, I said, "That's my boyfriend." Benjamin looked at the TV, inspecting Justin Timberlake, then looked over at me, sitting on the couch in my flannel pajamas and said, "Yeah. You wish. Good luck with that, mom." Oh, out of the mouths of babes! I bust out laughing because even at the tender age of five, Benjamin was fully aware that no middle-age mom had a shot with JT. Now, you may think that Benjamin was being rude or disrespectful I don't see it that way. I am not easily offended by my children. I have always found my kids to be very funny and light-hearted. We all love to laugh – that's kind of a theme in my house – and I almost never take offense to them making fun of me. Most of the time, they are my reality check. At the end of the day, it doesn't matter how pretty I may feel, or how much I may be gawking over some celebrity, to my kids I'm just a mom. And you know what? That's an AWESOME feeling.

Chapter 14

On Life and Loss

I THINK ONE OF THE REASONS WHY I ENJOY HAVING SO MANY kids is because of my own childhood. There are four of us in our family. I have an older brother, James, then me, and two younger sisters, Phyllis and Victoria. Growing up always felt like a party, lots of people, lots of noise, lots of chaos, and lots of love. Now, when all of our families get together it's pretty much the same as it was when I was younger, just more people and more noise. Family noise is the best noise. I have a very close relationship with each one of my siblings, all for different reasons. James and I enjoy each other's humor, Phyllis and I enjoy each other's advice, and Victoria and I enjoy each other similarities. Each relationship exposes me to a deeper understanding of myself, and a better understanding of our family. No matter what our differences may be, we all hold the same strong work ethic, determination, and a strong sense of the importance and value of family. No matter what ever happens in our lives, they will always be my first and best friends.

This point became abundantly clear to me when my father was dying of cancer. All of us were there, surrounding him. With our hands locked together and prayers whispered from our lips, we all witnessed his last moment of life. He was on his way to the gates of heaven. We knew that we needed to experience his passing as a family in order to eventually heal and grow from it. Although this event was devastating for all of us, it will forever be remembered as something that we experienced together, and we will never be alone through our journey to heal.

I have included a very personal entry from my own journal that I wrote after my father died. I feel the need to share this. It is written as I wrote it, in its rawest form, as the writing style is a stream of consciousness. The words show a sense of the heartache, strife, and healing from that time. For me, it is important to stay true to the facts, which helped me grow into the mother I am today; therefore, I have kept the entry within its full integrity.

Below is the unedited entry of my journal which I wrote the weeks following my father's death. It is something so raw and all over the place, but it's all true, and it changed the way I viewed life from that moment on:

fear, shock, sadness, relief.........these are the words I would use to describe the past couple of weeks of my life. I have been profoundly changed by my father's death and I wonder if I will ever be whole again. On Thursday Jan 5, 2006, I watched in terror my father die, my siblings and I begged him to come back, screamed in anger and utter disbelief not to leave us behind.... my sister Victoria shook and cried about the unfairness of her chronological order in our family, she began vomiting in the corner of the room, I watched as my sister Phyllis cried and screamed in pure disbelief, I too, could not believe my eyes........ I remember watching my mother stand at the end of the bed as her children begged God for mercy - she for just a moment watched her family be torn apart, before she was able to react with the same disbelief, anger and sadness the rest of us portrayed. That is not how our story ends though.... my brother James saved him that night.......forced my father's frail body to come back - my dad's only son screamed for him to focus on his voice, to fight the urge of death and with one sentence he did that, "dad, you come back, and I will name my son Henry...." At about that time, the doctors came in and marveled in our sadness and told us "Girls, he is gone, calm down..." At that point my dad's blood pressure was 30/20 and the situation looked grim, but in amazement we watched those numbers go up until he stabilized again......... as we held hands and prayed around my dad's hospital bed, we began our family theme song: "The Sun Will Come Out Tomorrow," from the movie *Annie*, remarkably, my dad took off his oxygen mask and began: "bet your bottom dollar that tomorrow they'll be sun...." My dad was back, for the hundredth time, he beat the odds, he returned from the dead, he fooled us all.... After a grueling hour of watching my dad's blood pressure drop, eyes roll in the back of his head, body jerk and literally watch life escape him, he was back, we celebrated, rejoiced and with that, we were more confident than ever, my dad, our hero was going to make it....... Until the next time. The next day, Friday, January 6th, we were somewhat upbeat despite the havoc the night before played on us... we thought, he beat death for a reason, that God must have a plan for him, that he was that one percent survival, that we proved his doctors wrong and that that he would be written in medical books to be envied by so many others. We were so confident that he would be fine that we persuaded my mom to go home to take a shower and we would stay with him. Within a half hour of that, the nurse asked us to leave so that the cleaning people could mop the floors, I was hesitant but since we had all camped out for so many days with my dad, I thought it would spruce things up and we could at least have a somewhat clean smell emanating from the room. My sisters and I sat outside the ICU chatting with my dad's friend, Mike, bragging about how strong my dad is and how badly he wants to live and how much he loves us…. My brother and Uncle Joe went to get everyone a bite to eat. I remember the nurse coming out trying to keep herself composed when she said, "your father needs you." I remember looking through the glass window in the ICU and to my horror, my dad's jerking body was there dying yet again. We ran in, and this time my sisters and I were a bit more composed, but still we begged him to come back. I remember hoping my brother would come back soon and that Mike would reach him quickly to tell him to come back up. My most vivid memory of that time was hoping that my mom would get back soon. She deserved more than anyone to be there if this was to be my father's last moments. She was the one to stick by him for 35 years of marriage, take care of him, to love him, she needed to get there and quick. My brother and Uncle came rushing in and again, like a big brother does, James took charge, "Dad come back, please come back." His blood pressure dropped and again was working its way back up…At around the same time my mother came rushing in asking, "what happened?" Again, death tried to take my dad and again, he came back…. This time though, we weren't so confident about my dad's survival…. Was he going to beat this, or were we just holding him back from the inevitable?

That night my dad had many visitors. We could tell by the look on their faces that they were coming to say goodbye. I wanted to punch them all and yell in their faces and tell them that they were wrong. My dad, my Superman, would never do that to us. Instead, we stood resilient, smiled and thanked them all for coming. Little did we know how desperately wrong we were. Once everyone left we were so sure that tomorrow would bring much needed hope, as we planned to meet with his doctors on a plan of action. He clearly understood my statement. "Doctor, dying is not an option for my dad, so give us something else…."

That night, together, our family gathered around my father and washed his naked body and brushed his silver hair. We brushed his teeth and dressed him for his night-time sleep, believing that one more was ahead of us. Our family, together, changed his bed sheets, made his bed, freshened his water, and talked about tomorrow. We had no idea that our preparation for our dad was actually his was preparation to pass. In the early morning of that night he lost his battle with cancer. Later, our comfort was felt by the love and closeness of all of us being together. I was very lucky to have my best friends as my true family unit. We stuck together and took care of our dad and each other.

Later that evening, I remember glancing at the clock from my spot on the window sill. It was 10:50. I wanted to get a couple of hours sleep because the night before was restless for all of us. My mom went up to each one of us and gave us a goodnight kiss like she did when we were children. I remember feeling happy that we were all together in that room, even though we knew the ending. Just as I was getting comfortable (well, as comfortable as you get sleeping on the window sill) I looked at the clock again and it was 11:03 pm.

Within minutes my dad said "oh no, not again" …… and started convulsing. It was happening again, and this time all the begging in the world would not save him. That was the beginning of the end. As a family, we decided earlier that day to change the DNR to resuscitate because my other siblings thought we should give him every opportunity to live.

When his body started convulsing uncontrollably we rushed out of his room for help-- within seconds a rush of doctors came in, and I remember screaming, "Please save my daddy..." The lights got so bright and the chaos in the room was so stressful-- we were waiting outside of his room, watching the events unfold when the doctor came out and told us to let him go, that saving him would be cruel... he would be brain dead and then we would have to make the decision to pull the plug. We all agreed that we should take the doctor's advice and just stand by him and watch him take his last breaths. Little did we know, that is not how peaceful it would be for him. It was a violent, horrific five-hour ordeal, that has scarred my memory forever.

Even now, I cannot find the courage to write them down......... tidbits of memories swirl around my head every day: *singing Bobby McGee; You're crowd'en me; Why you all looking around like I'm dying or somethin'? Then he smirked, Jesus Christ, I gave him a left hook then a right hook, you're not taking me from my babies; Six people, I'm taking six people, that sucks; But mommy will be left all alone; open the door, open the door; I'm going now, shut the door, it's beautiful.*

My father's last breath occurred at 4:38 am. I heard a huge crack and as all the gases expelled from of his body. After each of us gave him one last kiss and said goodbye, we gathered up all of our belongings that had been collected from a week's worth of being by his side and walked out of the hospital room. I remember the staff clapping, and me thinking *don't clap for us - we failed him, he died anyway.* We were defeated, we fought death, and death won. Now what? After that, things were a blur, but all of us marveled at what we had just been through and bragged of my dad's strength and courage -- it was a story we thought needed to be told to everyone.

I remember falling asleep in my dad's bed with my sisters and awaking to a house full of people. The food, the hugs, the sympathetic eyes, it was all just so surreal. The next day we had to make arrangements and I remember thinking that my father's dead body was somewhere in the building getting ready for a showing. The thought made me sick. Was this all really happening to us? That night my siblings and I were putting together photos and collages for my dad's wake, and it felt like we were kids working on a school project, trying to outdo the others' work. We have the ability to stay close and laugh in the most devastating situations. The next day was the wake and I had a nervous feeling in my stomach. How would my dad look? How would people act? How are we supposed to take on the role of our personal grief? This was all so new to us. We were the family people always looked up to and never pitied.

Before we left for the first viewing I was walking past the front door of my parent's house when I heard a lot of noise. I looked outside to find about 100 black birds loudly squawking on our front lawn. I could barely think straight. I called upon the rest of my family to see this incredible event. Never before had I seen anything like this in my 25 years at this house. Without warning, they all began to shit all over the place – all at the same time. The squawking got louder and louder and then they flew away in complete silence. Moments later, they all returned, and the noise was deafening. As we stood there watching and listening to this mass of blackbirds squawking and shitting, they abruptly flew away again in complete silence, and never returned. I have no doubt that it was a sign from my father that he was okay, and that he was still with us. Those loud and shitting blackbirds were really quite comforting for all of us.

The summer prior to my father's death, we had a serious conversation. I asked him if he thought he would beat cancer. For the first time, he said, "No, this is going to kill me." He had been battling the disease for years by then, and I knew he was tired, both mentally and physically. I straight out asked him that if there was a heaven, could he please give me a sign, that I could not or would not second guess, to let me know he was going to be okay. After his death, he gave me that gift of knowing that heaven is for real, and from that my faith has grown. My father's final lesson to me was proof that there is life after death, and that he will always be present.

What I learned from my father's life and of his death, was that nothing lasts forever. Embrace every day and enjoy every moment. Most importantly, I learned that after I am gone my children will judge me on the mother that I was, the attention that I gave them, the love that I showed, and the dedication I had for them. My father's life and his death has forced me to become very aware of the impact that I will make on my children for the rest of their lives. Whether I am physically alive or not, my existence will forever form their lives; that is a responsibility and honor I take seriously.

Afterthought: Remember that brush I used to brush my father's hair that morning when we all gathered around him to get him ready for the day? I have it in the bottom drawer of my dresser, with his hair still in it. Sometimes I find myself going to that drawer to open it, just to see that brush, a loving reminder of my father and my family.

Chapter 15

Life's Adventures

MAYBE IT'S BECAUSE MY DAD DIED YOUNG, OR MAYBE IT'S because I'm a free spirit at heart, but so many of the little details of life really don't bother me. Skipping school to spend time with my kids just happens sometimes, bedtime at my house is arbitrary – when you're tired, go to bed, and dessert before dinner is not a crime. I don't get myself worked up over these sorts of things. I want my kids to look back with fondness on their years under my roof. I want them to remember the times they had fun, loved, and laughed more than any rules that needed to be followed or punishments that weren't given. I may be free spirited, but I have taught my children to understand that for every decision, there is a consequence – good, bad, or indifferent. The 9 pm runs for ice cream, the late-night dance parties, the snuggle time and board games. All of these equals memories that my children will hold onto for a lifetime, like I do. They will have learned how to love and live peacefully in a family. I want them to remember their place in our home as a happy adventure.

I have learned from my own childhood and I have learned from my children. I hope when they look back on their upbringing, they will describe it as fun. Lots and lots of fun. I loved raising my little ones with fun. Because they were so close in age, what was fun for one, was equally as fun for the others. Because I'm not hung up on the traditional "discipline" and rules, it leaves a lot of extra time to just be silly. In fact, on any given night, you could drive past my home and see all six of us hanging around the kitchen table at 10 or 11 o'clock at night, talking, laughing, sometimes even having a dance party, over a freshly delivered pizza pie. Did I mention that it could be a school night? My philosophy with my family is to capture fun when the fun moment strikes! Not getting hung up on bedtime and appropriate meal times, I have had the best conversations and the most fun as a family around that table late at night. It's not every night, not even every week, but when it happens I embrace it with every ounce of love. As I look around that table at their sleepy eyes and smiling faces, I listen to the cacophony of chatter with everyone talking at once. I just know that for my family there is so much to be learned and so much to be grateful for on any random weeknight at 10 pm when we are gathered around the kitchen table eating pizza. Whether it's poking fun at one another, laughing about what may have happened at school that day, or playing a few games of Uno, I consider those nights sacred.

I know this in unconventional, and by now you are holding your breath and gasping for air. You can't figure out how a woman with four kids has her household run smoothly and peacefully, and her answer is to eat pizza at 10 pm on a school night. No. That is not the answer. The answer and the secret is to create circumstances and activities for the entire family. As your children grow, it will be easier for them to get along with their siblings. My point is, there is nothing better than feeling the bond grow between all of us.

From a very early age, I had a rule in my house that I adopted from a friend who had kids older than ours. Our dear friend, Michael, had a great story about his experience with his kids and how they all coexist in peace. I loved his idea and carried that into our home. In our house, no one is allowed to put anyone else in our family down, including themselves. From an early age my kids were raised in a children-centered environment where they were not exposed to stressed-out parents. My children knew that as soon as they walked through that door they were in very safe territory. No fights. No yelling. No acting out. It just wasn't like that. It turned out that everyone seems to like each other, so they didn't have to worry about being bullied or hurt.

We can't protect our children from a lot of stuff that happens outside our home, but we can make it an absolute rule that we treat one another with kindness inside our home. It begins with a simple 'please pass the salt and pepper' to respecting that others have to use the bathroom. When they forget, I remind them that we are family, and no matter what, we stick together. Our name means something to us. It is something we honor. And then it happens, they truly understand the importance and power of family. And pride: they make me proud on a daily basis.

Recently, Emma was sick with a terrible viral infection. I knew she had to have been feeling pretty miserable for her to miss school, and to miss the school pep rally. When Benjamin attended the pep rally and noticed that his sister missed it, he gathered up all the balloons he could find. As I pulled up to his school that day to pick him up, he was having trouble holding onto them. When I asked him about it, he said, "You'll see."

As soon as we got home, he went straight to find Emma who was laid out on the coach, and announced, "Introducing Emma Morandi!" and threw the balloons at her. Her smile said it all. Benjamin's thoughtfulness proved the importance of their relationship.

As easygoing as I am, being unkind to each other will not be tolerated under our roof. It is important to me, and to them, to know that we all have one other's back. When times are good, we celebrate together and when one of us struggles, we are all there for support.

So many have lost that sense of family now because they are so darn busy. I find most are busy outside the home with things that have nothing to do with the inside of their home. Where's the balance? When you look at your own lifestyle, how much time do you spend doing things outside your family? How much time are you spending inside your home? How much time are you spending with each of your children? How much time are you spending with your family? How much time are you spending with your husband or significant other? See what I mean? When you slice it out into a pie, what are the percentages? Now, the bigger question is, are you satisfied with how you spend your time?

To understand what it means to grow a family is to know that it begins in your home. So, make it comfortable and peaceful and active and fun and enlightening and lots and lots of fun.

Many rules that parents in general impose on their children are not as important to me because they have no value. I am not strict about curfews, hanging out with friends, and doing fun stuff. I am, however, a stickler about manners; that is my no tolerance zone. I am appalled at the times when I observe other children behaving in a way that would be completely unacceptable in my home. I believe in please and thank you, greeting adults with a hand shake when you walk into a room, and conducting yourself in a way that shows respect. Every time they step foot out of our house they are representing the Morandi family. That is their one rule. Each one works with that. They have learned to thank their coaches, be a good teammate, be respectful at school, and be a proud member of our community. This is where they test their own limits and boundaries and learn about cause and effect. We get through it; hopefully, they learn something, and we move on. However, no matter what, I expect my children to always be polite, kind, and show respect. Others take notice. They see when children treat others differently; some with respect and some with disrespect. Showing disrespect can lead to disaster. I hope that my children continue to consistently do what I expect them to, even when I'm not looking. I tell them all the time that their confidence, respect, and kindness will make them stand out among their peers.

My house has always been the "go-to" house. The house where all the friends gather, the parties are held, and the sleepovers happen. Honestly, I don't mind it at all. Our house has earned a certain reputation to be where everyone hangs out, snacks on munchies, and socializes. These friends of my children would stay for hours and hours, laughing and talking about what's going on, watching movies, or playing games. The best part was that I knew exactly where my kids were.

Okay, it's not that simple because the price I pay for being the "home base" house can get quite expensive. Our food bill is definitely more than what a six-member family can eat. But to me, it is an investment that is worth making. Be stocked up on all the good snacks in exchange to breathing a little easier knowing where the kids are. That is called money well spent. It probably costs me close to 100 bucks more a week in groceries. But let's face it, it's less than bail money! (That's a joke. We're having fun, remember?) They are safe, and out of trouble, and I know where they are. Most parents would never allow so many kids together at once in their house. Kids getting together can put a strain on the family with the messes they make, the snacks they devour, and their loud shenanigans going on sometimes into the wee hours of the morning.

I take a different approach. I know where my kids are, I know what they are doing. I know who they are with, and a mess is just a mess that can be easily cleaned up. I'll admit when my daughter asked to invite 45 teenagers to her birthday party I was a little nervous. How could I handle 45 teenagers? I bought all their favorite processed food: plenty of chips of all kinds, a plethora of soda, and candy galore. Keep them fed, keep them happy. The day of her party I made sure to move all the furniture, precious glassware, pictures, and anything easily breakable. Then I removed the soft white rug from the living room floor. Sure, it was a little inconvenient, but so is rug shopping. I knew in the long run, accommodating the teenagers was the best choice.

When all the teenagers started piling into my home, I watch them intermingle with each other, at first a little shy, but eventually they all got comfortable. It was nice to watch teenagers mingle within a group when they think no parents are watching. Teenagers are a weird lot. Often, I find them fun to observe. Many people think negatively of teenagers and are afraid of them but let me be the first to tell you. Teenagers are incredibly interesting and complex. The more you know about them, the more the world makes sense. I am quietly in the background, checking out their antics. There are shy girls in the corner, the more outgoing ones dancing, the boys showing off for the girls, and the occasional awkward glances between both the boys and girls. The party went on for four hours and there were a lot of laughs, whispering, dancing, and fun. During times like these, it was a pleasure experiencing teenage life through my adult eyes.

When the party was over and the cleanup was done, my daughter made it a point to thank me for being so cool. Being called cool by your teenager is probably the highest compliment you can receive. I'll take it. My kids feel comfortable enough in their own home to invite their friends to spend time here. They are not embarrassed by their parents, and they have nothing to hide about their friends and what they do to have fun. My children know that I will always make sure there is plenty of snacks, drinks, and comfort. I want them to think our home as a safety net. A place where they feel at home, in the truest sense. A place where the outside world doesn't matter, a place where they can just be themselves, safely and without judgment. I feel good that my children know they can come to us with just about anything. If they are in trouble, I want to know that I am the first call that they will make. Time and time again they have made that call, and time and time again they know that regardless of the time or the inconvenience, we will be there. They know in our home it's okay to make mistakes, it's okay to fail, as long as it is followed by learning, growing, experiencing, and moving forward.

I have so many wonderful memories with my children. I was never one to need my husband to come along on all of our adventures. He was busy with his career, providing for us and making a name for himself. Instead of missing out on many valuable and fun experiences, I just went without him. I would take all four children, from newborn to the age of seven, to movies, theme parks, and museums, both in and out of state. There is a wonderful, yet terribly dirty, establishment that all my kids loved: Sesame Place Theme Park in Pennsylvania. It is a lot of what you would expect: crying kids, dirty diapers, frazzled parents, and many memories in the making. I would take the 2 ½ -hour drive over the Throgs Neck Bridge, through the New York City traffic to Sesame Place a couple of times during the summer. I would manage all four children, all the exploding diapers, the temper tantrums, and the chaos that goes along with it all. I will tell you that although it was not always easy, it gave me a sense of power and control to teach my children that in order to partake in these activities we all had to work together. The older they got, my older kids would help with their younger siblings, and the younger children understood their boundaries. Had it not been for their cooperation and my impeccable patience level, those trips would have never been able to happen.

In many ways, teaching my children to travel at a young age also taught them what it meant to be part of our family. We experienced many fun adventures together, but each defined him or herself as a part of the family unit. Each person in our family had a place and a responsibility to live up to. Although unspoken, each person in our family knew where they stood in our family, and that all of them were valued. William is the creative one, the kid who made up all the fun games, out of essentially nothing. Emma is the organizer, keeping everyone in line and included in the activities. Benjamin is the one who always takes it to the next level and pushes the limits to make the activity extra ordinary. Matthew, the youngest, and believe it or not, the bossiest, makes sure his voice is always heard and that everything is always fair. Each child knows their strengths, and knows they have a voice in our family, and that those strengths are constantly encouraged and celebrated. That's why traveling for us has always been essential. We would take the kids on long plane rides from the time they were infants. For us, traveling helped us experience as a family life outside of our home environment. We have taken so many amazing trips as a family, and those are the times I treasure most. One time, when we were away in Europe we were sitting at a British pub, and I remember feeling at that moment, that life was just perfect. I was filled with gratitude and love and when I looked around the table at my four children and husband I thought, "Wow! This is the life I always dreamed of, and the kids I always hoped for. Lucky, lucky me."

Just then, Matthew tripped, spilled his drink on William's lap, Benjamin jumped to back away, and ended up elbowing Emma. Then they all started to bicker about what just occurred, and I sat there hysterically laughing, thinking, *oh, for fuck sake,* I love these people! We had many great adventures on that summer trip to Europe. We spent 18 days in three countries. My kids learned to navigate the subway system in England, gained an understanding of danger when there was a potential terror attack in Paris, and grasped the concept of their surroundings in Barcelona. On one particular day in Paris, we were seated outside of this quaint restaurant having a wonderful meal. We were all huddled around the table, laughing and talking among ourselves. I had a bright yellow bag that I kept by my foot between both me and my husband for safe keeping. At one point, I wasn't paying attention and these two impeccably dressed men reached down and snatched it, unbeknownst to any of us. Emma turned her head slightly long enough to see a glimpse of my yellow bag in one of the man's hands. Without thinking, she shouted, "Mom, isn't that your bag?" Benjamin, the feistiest of all, jumped out of his seat and began chasing these two adult men down the streets of Paris. Immediately, I thought, "*Oh, for fuck sake,* this little lunatic is going to get himself killed! I jumped up to chase Benjamin, with Peter right behind me. The men must have been rattled enough, because they dropped the bag with all of my belongings still intact. As Peter and I continued to chase after them, we entrusted Benjamin to go back with the other kids. As we were focused on finding the perpetrators, and screaming profanities that I will not repeat here, but you can be sure that there were some F-bombs for sure. At some point, Peter looked at me and said, "What are we doing? We got our bag back, why are we still chasing these guys?" I had no idea. Then it dawned on me that, oh shit… *for fuck sake,* our four children are sitting alone around the block and this could be just a ploy to kidnap them! Luckily, everyone was fine and we replayed the scene for the rest of the night. The more we laughed and told our stories the more exaggerated the experience became. It makes for a great narrative, and a lesson that not everyone seems to be who they appear. That Benjamin, though. He has my sense of fight in him which could either be a curse or a blessing, I guess time will tell.

Originally, our trip was for 16 days in Europe, but we missed our plane. Before I continue, I want you to know that I think that Peter is great. He is organized, and our travel arrangements are almost always to perfection. The day we were leaving to return home, our arrangements to the airport were anything but perfect or organized. There's nothing like 16 days on a European vacation; but honestly, we were all looking forward to sleeping in our own beds and eating our familiar foods. We were also looking forward to our very anticipated Long Island summer. If you've never been on the Island during the summer, you are missing out on a lot.

Unfortunately, going home was not to be our destiny on that day. Our cab driver arrived 45 minutes late to take us to the airport, and then we were stuck in a gay pride parade. Realizing we were going nowhere by staying in the cab, all six of us – you know: mom, dad, William, Emma, Matthew, and Benjamin – jumped out of the cab and ran through the streets of London weaving between cars, up and down countless steps, and squeezing into subway cars to get to the airport. After hours of racing to make our plane, we were exhausted and fifteen minutes too late to board. I looked at my kids' heads drop in despair, and knew I had a choice to make. I could begin an argument with Peter, blaming him for not getting the cab earlier, (even though I said to), I could have joined their pity party, I could have easily freaked out, or I could have hysterically laughed at the situation. Which way do you think I went? I knew this was a perfect learning moment for the Morandi family - on many levels. The first is that things don't always turn out the way you want, and you have to learn to roll with change. There will be unexpected times where you need to adapt and regroup and make the best of the situation. Here we were, sitting on the floor of the airport with no place to go. We were tired, hungry, and eager to get home. Even though this sounds like a grim situation, I was looking for the lesson that we could learn. That lesson was: Preparation. We knew what time the flight was leaving, and we simply did not leave enough wiggle room for traffic, or any other unforeseen events, like in our case, a gay pride parade and the massive amount of people in London that day. The lesson that our family learned that day was that we should not always assume that things will work out for us, even when we are not prepared. And the bigger lesson I learned that day, is wow! gay pride people sure know how to party! What an incredible show of pride and happiness and laughter. You know the way parades are.

Another great family adventure was when we took a family trip to California. It was the summer of 2016 and Emma convinced me to take her to some YouTube convention. Emma and I flew out first to attend the convention, and the boys met us out there a couple of days later. We visited Los Angeles and then went to the iconic city of San Francisco – the kids enjoyed the famous *In and Out* burger chain restaurant, the rolling hills, and all the small boutique shops. The bonus was that the weather was beautiful. Good thing, because we decided to take a bike tour through the streets to get a better feel of the city. We love to travel to new places and get the vibe or the feel. Do you ever get that way? We wanted to go through the streets, look at things people who live there look at every day. We want to eat in their restaurants. We thought that the bike tour would be the best way to do that. At first, I was a little hesitant because Matthew was seven and Benjamin nine. I wasn't sure if they would be able to navigate the winding roads and the hilly mountains; not to mention the busy roads and the unfamiliar surroundings. Since our family is always up for an adventure, I agreed with Peter that this would be a good family tour for everyone and we would get some good exercise in doing it. Matthew went on a tandem bike with Peter so that he would be able to keep up with the rest of us and we could stay together throughout the tour. I would be lying if I said I wasn't nervous about looking ahead and seeing my kids ahead of us, peddling full speed through the roads that they shared with cars, other bikers, and pedestrians. I took a breath, said a prayer to keep us all safe, and kept a watchful eye as best I could. For the entire two-hour tour, the kids rode with delight, and we saw so many amazing sights. We stopped off at a little shop where we were able to buy some snacks and cold drinks, and of course, our traditional souvenirs. Despite my reservations, we were all having a great time and were excited about all the new information we learned about San Francisco. At the bottom of the hill we had someone take a picture of the six of us with the San Francisco Bridge behind in the background. As we traveled up the hill, closer to the bridge, we saw the beautiful and inviting San Francisco Bay. The newness of the moment was mesmerizing. I was a little ahead of Benjamin and told him to follow me carefully because there were a lot of other bikers on the bridge. Within minutes, I heard a crash and knew instinctively that it was him. I threw my bike to the side of the busy path and went running for my baby boy. Once there, his knees were bloody and he was obviously shaken up. A woman who did not speak fluent English was beside him, apologizing to him, saying that she lost control of her bike and went into his lane and crashed into him. Lucky for all of us, especially Benjamin, he just had some scrapes and bruises. Like a champ, he continued on the tour without any complaints and with just a little soreness because he knew a promise was a promise and there was ice cream at the end. Every time we see a picture of that bridge we all remember that day and how it could have been disastrous. What we all learned from that experience is that we can control our own actions and be as careful as possible, but we cannot control others. Be ready for unforeseen accidents and hope that when one does hit, you are able to brush yourself off, get back up, and continue on your journey. And consider getting an ice cream cone along the way.

Chapter 16

Failure – The Greatest of Life Lessons

Part of life is failure. We learn all sorts of important lessons from failure. Failure to prepare, failure to try, failure to commit, failure to listen, and most important, failure to accept that failure is one of the greatest life lessons. I would like to think that failure is nothing more than another experience to help move me along on my journey.

For as long as I can remember I wanted to become a writer. I was always too afraid to expose myself in such a vulnerable way, but deep down in my heart, I always longed to write a book. As a child with severe learning disabilities, the thought of writing seemed impossible. That never stopped my desire or will to write, but I was never quite ready to commit myself to the challenge. I love books. I love the smell of them, the feel of them, the words in them, and the way they fit in my hands. There is something about books, they do something to me that I can't quite explain. It's a feeling of hope, imagination, and perseverance. As I moved through the grades, I couldn't catch on to reading. More than anything, I wanted the words to come easy to me. I wanted to read, I tried to read, I just couldn't figure out the words on the paper. I was in a reading class until the sixth grade. Year after year, the teachers wanted to hold me back, but my mother would fight for me and demand my advancement to the next grade level. She would argue, "This child has a book in her hand every day. How am I supposed to look my child in the eye and say she's not good enough? That her best is just not good enough, at the mere age of seven years old?" My mother won the fight and I would carry on to the next grade continuing my pitiful reading skills and low self-esteem.

This experience had a very profound effect on me. In fact, it shaped me into becoming the woman I am today. Watching her speak on my behalf made me realize that all of us, even children, have rights. My mother taught me to be my own advocate. I am one of those lucky daughters who is blessed with a perfect mother. She's beautiful inside, and on the outside, she is stunning. As physically gorgeous as she is, she is kind, patient, loving, and has a fantastic sense of humor. The greatest thing I can ever say about my mother is that she never gave up on me. When I was a child and struggled every day in school, she would patiently guide me and cheer me on to do my best. I couldn't read, I couldn't write, I had trouble in math, and I was constantly on the verge of falling behind. In grade school the reading teachers constantly asked to leave me back a grade. My mother knew that leaving me back despite my effort would crush me, and she would not allow it. I always worked hard, trying to improve my reading and get on grade level, but no matter how hard I tried, I could never quite get there. The result of that was low self-esteem, which also lead to finding opportunities to isolate myself from others. My mother's fight for me to excel and move onto the next grade level was heroic. She couldn't understand why my teachers couldn't see my potential like she could. Her perseverance as my advocate stuck with me my entire life. I hear my mother's voice, "Just keep going, keep trying. All anyone can expect is your best." She never compared me or made me feel badly about my academic deficiencies. She would remind me that some people were good in math, some were good in science or English, and everyone is different and that's what makes the world go around. My mother believed in me when no one else did, and for that I will forever be grateful. If it had it not been for her, I probably would not be writing this book now. She was my voice, my confidence, and my determination, until I found a way through maturity to be my own advocate. I also knew I would have to work twice as hard as the rest of the students, and I developed a terrific work ethic. I knew that I would have to fight self-esteem issues, and therefore, form my own confidence so that others will believe that I was worthy.

I wanted desperately to be smart so that one day I could go to college and join as many clubs that I could, knowing that my SAT scores would not help my admission. Eventually, I did get caught up in reading and that was a glorious time, because then I flourished. Not only did I love to read, it became my passion. All through my life, I have been motivated by a fear of failure. Failure was my motivation to do the New York City Marathon, to complete the Tobay Triathlon despite having a panic attack during it, and eventually completing the Quassy Half Ironman. During all the training of these events, especially the half Ironman, that old voice in my head kept creeping back into my chatter saying stuff like I was not good enough. About this time, instead of pushing books completely out of my life because others said it wasn't working for me was one option. But the thought that I will never read or be good enough was shouting every insecurity about failure, defeat, and embarrassment. That voice tried to convince me that I was not strong enough, brave enough, or good enough to accomplish anything. At one point, I silently mustered up every excuse to get out of it. People will understand if you drop out, or you have an auto immune disease, or you have four young kids to care for. It is obvious to the innocent eye that you probably don't have the time to do anything more than what you are doing right now and for the next 15 years. While this is true, as each year passed, I got a little smarter, and now if I say I don't have time, it's because it is not at the top of my priority list. Unless you value what you are going to devote your time to, it will never happen. Perhaps a little part of me wanted to listen to that voice, but the bigger part, the part that will always persevere and has an inherit determination of a survivor, would never allow me to quit. There's something inside of me, something that just snaps. When I make a decision, it's going to happen, no matter what the sacrifice. I can't be held down for long. After the half Ironman, I got a tattoo. It says, "I refuse to sink," with an anchor at the bottom. It represents that no matter the circumstances or the adversity that may be against me, I will always persevere. I will always be terrified, and I will do it anyway. Also, I have a tattoo on my right forearm that says the word "gratitude" with an infinity symbol. It is a reminder of the immense gratitude I have for this life, the life that I fought to create, and the life I once thought would always be just a dream. The words tattooed on my arm are not just words, but actions.

Be grateful. Have gratitude. You have the life that you dreamed, hold on to it, enjoy it, submerge yourself in this life. I appreciate that daily reminder when I look down and know that I have so much to be grateful for. On my left forearm there is a key with the word "love" on top of it. It represents the key to life is love, but also that I hold the key to my own happiness. When I got this tattoo, I was depressed and needed to remind myself that I had to make me happy before anyone or anything else in our family could be happy. Originally, I had just the key, but later added the word *love* on top of it because what I learned through some dark times is that love is always the key. Have love, show love, be love.

Besides many and unexpected obstacles, writing this book was extra difficult. I am a person who always needs to be in perpetual motion. Always doing, always completing, constantly on the go. I have talked myself into believing that I must be productive at all times. Taking the time to sit down and put my thoughts together to create my vision was a challenge.

Choosing to not do laundry, putting off errands, or tidying the house and instead fulfilling my goals was a life changing experience. For the first time in my adult life, I chose me, and it was empowering. It took years for me to have the courage to finally commit to this process. Men generally do not have these issues, although I'm sure there are always some exceptions. My husband had no problem fulfilling all of his dreams, going after everything he wanted and becoming a successful businessman. He finds the time to train and compete in half Ironman races, socializes with friends, and even meditates. Yet, I felt continual guilt that came like a force to my soul and made me doubt if I was good enough, if I was available enough for my kids, if I was loving enough to my husband, if I was attentive enough to my friends and family. So many of these raw emotions come from being that little child in that big classroom whirling with doubt and embarrassment. Now though, I am an adult who is able to tame those emotions and has the confidence to take risks despite the possibility of failure. Life has taught me that failure is just an experience and one of the best life lessons taught.

Experience has taught me to be humble, kind, and quiet. As each year passes I've become more introverted. Quieter, more observant, and less vocal. It's not that I have less to say, nor do I want to engage less, but I am more thoughtful with my words. I am now more attuned to my feelings, and less willing to expose them to others. With age, I have realized that I don't always have to speak my opinion, people don't always need to know my business, and I don't always have to share my secrets. As I get older I've learned boundaries. What I've noticed is that often, people who are a bit insecure are usually louder than the people around them. They need the attention, they need the validation, and they need the noise. I know that when I was in college, I would be that one looking for the attention. I am no longer in that season of my life. I enjoy quiet, more deep relationships, and better conversations. Reading and writing and spending time with intimate groups of friends is what I value most. Overall, I get to experience the best of others. I generally get to surround myself with people who are positive and full of life. They are hopeful and give off positive vibes. I thrive in environments where I sense good energy. Having people with like minds who enjoy the small treasures of life is the ultimate.

My running group is made up of women who enjoy the benefits of a good run. We chat weekly about the good and bad from that particular week. We look to each other for advice and as a support system. Our time together is full of laughter and fun and theorizing about many issues from politics to family to deep conversations. We are honest and open with one another and are able to talk freely without judgment or tension. This group of friends are the same ones who meet once a month to have dinner, drinks, laughter, and friendship. It took me many years to find my "tribe," the people who I can confide in, laugh with, cry with, and know that they will always be there - cheering me on or wiping away my tears. All these people have one important thing in common. They all share an excitement for life. They are all curious, interesting, and full of positive energy. Being around them forces and encourages me to be my best self: to think broader, hold onto faith more, be more empathetic, find compassion, and to always see life as a fun adventure.

Days gone are loud people, loud parties, and noise for the sake of noise. People that do not add a certain value to my inner circle are no longer welcome. It does not make them bad people and it does not mean that I don't care for them or enjoy them. It simply means that my circle is now filled with people who have the same priorities, zest for life, and abundance of knowledge in order for me to be at my best. I no longer have patience for small talk, gossip, or irrelevant negative behavior. It's funny how you grow, you find what is important, who is important, and how you can revolve around certain people in order for you to evolve. In fact, I find myself driving without any radio and watching such little television, because what used to be background noise to me is now outside noise, which is really just noise. I don't need or want irrelevant noise around my energy. Talk shows and news channels babble on so I avoid them, just like I avoid arguments, confrontations, and any other negative energy that tries to interrupt my positive flow.

I want my legacy to be of kindness, love, joy, and filled with peace. If I surround myself with noise, negativity, and gossip I cannot stay focused on my journey. I know that now. I will no longer expose myself to anything less than I know was meant to be. I trust myself, I believe in myself, and I am comfortable with myself.

Each of us has a uniqueness, something that cannot be replicated from person to person. There is something special in all of us. We all have different talents, different desires, different dreams, and different hopes. I have so many different curves within my soul. I am witty, but I am also a loner; a homebody with a dash of wild; independent, yet a caretaker; confident, yet doubting; laid-back, but structured; ambitious, but settled; competitive, yet only with myself; caring, yet skeptical. There are so many different layers in all of us and depending on the circumstances, or our current mood; we never quite know what we'll get. That's the beauty of humans, that's the beauty of life, the unexpected. It's not until we are comfortable within our own skin that we can fully understand this.

Through example, I try to teach my children that all the highs and lows in life, all the strengths and weaknesses we possess, and all the good and bad we experience will only last for a season. We often forget who we are because we get caught up in life's challenges. When we are true to ourselves, we are true to our children, our spouse, our community, and the world. I wish it didn't take so long to achieve comfort within our own skin. People spend their entire lives not being comfortable with who they are, which leads to many years of confusion, depression, and anxiety. Part of the adventure in life is to search through the journey of who you are and what you want to be. Once you discover your true self, celebrate all that comes with who you really are. I hope that my children get there sooner than I did so that they will feel content and happiness sooner than I did and for a far longer time.

Many of us will lose and find ourselves several times within our lifetime. It's part of growth, it's part of the journey. It's not a time to run, it is a time to embrace the experience. You need a certain amount of self-reflection to truly appreciate this. At times, it can be very frustrating, and you make mistakes, and look back on that season of your life with a little bit of regret. The important part is to remember what you learned. For there are lessons in everything if you are willing to learn and grow. You will be amazed at how many more opportunities life has been waiting to share with you.

I believe that with an open heart and an open mind, we can change the world in a grassroots way – one person at a time. The place where I find my clarity and solace is at the beach. In fact, that's where I do most of my writing. The beach gives me a sense of being one with nature. A place where I can clear my thoughts, think out loud, and feel at home. I love all the people here enjoying the same thing: the sound of the waves crashing, the cool water breeze, and the smell of the ocean. The beach is my "it" place, the place where I feel free, and happy. The place where I find gratitude and love, and the place that I feel most at ease. I realize that not everyone has the same fondness for the beach as me, but I think it's important that you have a place that you hold dear to your heart. A place where you can get into your own thoughts without interruption.

As much fondness as I have for the beach, that does not necessarily make up the perfect day for me. We all have our favorite places and favorite things. Fancy restaurants, simple picnics, a walk in the park, a skiing trip, a clear blue ocean. What is a perfect day for you? Perhaps a perfect day is one where I use the words, *for fuck sake,* maybe just once or twice. But if that were the case that would mean I probably wouldn't be around my kids. And not being around my children is usually not a good day, for totally different reasons. So, my day would certainly be filled with my children, which obviously would be filled with many *for fuck sakes*, which consequently would be filled with chaos. I find comfort in the chaos. I find the most joy and love in my life when I am in the eye of the storm with my kids. Admittedly, as much as I love the solitude of the beach, a perfect day for me would include being with my family, filled with laughter, love and chaos.

Chapter 17

Worry & Hope

MOTHERS DON'T STOP WORRYING, IT'S LIKE PART OF OUR DNA. Baby comes out and instantly we are worriers. It doesn't matter how big or how small or what it is, we will worry about it. Part of being a mother is enduring a certain amount of fear every day. It could be as simple as fear that your child is cold, didn't like the snack you packed, or misses you. But as they get older, the fear becomes more profound: do they feel happy enough? Are they confident enough? Then the fear becomes more terrifying. Will they make good decisions? Are they hanging out with the right people? Will they grow up to be financially secure and happy in their relationships? Yes, we worry. It never goes away. That what parents do. I work hard to keep my own ego out of parenting because I know the importance of my kids working through their bumps in the road. However, when I notice judgmental eyes looking and comparing, I begin to wonder, did my kid perform well enough at the baseball game? Did they make the honor society? Do they have enough friends? Are they with the right crowd? This worry comes at inopportune times, and I must keep reminding myself that it's fine; everything is fine. Normally, things like that don't bother me too much, but sometimes even I fall victim and the outside forces make it impossible to avoid that feeling of being not good enough.

I worry if my child has enough friends, if they are they are the right friends, if they're going to get into the college of their choice or get the job that they want, get the promotion that they hope for. I worry about their children. I hope their children will be healthy, I hope their spouses will be supportive, I hope, I hope, I worry, I worry. It's a non-stop cycle. And then I pause, I breathe, and realize that I can't control anything with worry. At the end of the day, I just want them safe, both emotionally and physically. I want to know when I'm an old lady rocking in my favorite rocking chair that I have four healthy, happy, safe children. Nothing else matters.

When I hear stories of parents losing their children, my insides start to rattle. How do you survive that? Yet I know firsthand that people do, that life eventually moves on… differently, but nonetheless, moves on. I have no control over what the universe will bring for me or my family. And guess what? Neither do you. None of us does, frankly. So, we can worry and we can hope and we can pray, but what we must do, and should do, is enjoy every second, every moment, and every worry-less situation that we get to experience. Accept the fact that you're going to worry. I wouldn't go so far as to say embrace it, but I will say, accept it. I know you know that some things are just out of your control, so *for fuck sake*, let it go.

Sometimes worry is impossible to avoid. Turn on the news, and you will get a strong whiff of it. Recently, there was a shooting at a high school. Seventeen innocent teenagers were at school, in their classes. The thought of one of my children being in such a horrific situation chills me to the bone. Not only do we have to worry about the surface stuff like good grades, good health, good friends, and good behavior, but now we have the daunting task of keeping our children safe in impossible situations. It's terrifying being a parent and knowing that at any time and at any place something unexpected can happen and be completely out of their control. One of the things I find helpful is to teach my children to have their wits about them, to understand their surroundings, to be aware of situations, and then I pray to God to keep my children safe.

As the years fly by and my children get older, my faith becomes stronger. I'm sure it's that way for many people. In these very crazy chaotic times, perhaps we can all use a little religion. Or maybe not. Maybe we just have to have faith. Faith in ourselves, faith in our community, and faith that the God I believe in is good, kind, and forgiving. More and more I seek out peace, tranquility, and God. Being connected with myself and with God makes me feel more in control, more with one about my own intentions, my own conscience, and my own well-being.

Unfortunately, even with the best intentions, and the greatest faith, we still cannot protect our children from everything. There was a scare at my children's school with a threat that a man was out to harm our children. The community was on alert and the school was vigilant to keep all of the students safe. I feel my insides shaking with all that is happening around me, things that are out of my control. Sometimes it is hard not to be on edge. I warn my children of being aware of their surroundings and to take appropriate precautions. I don't want them to ever view life in a negative or suspicious way, but I also want them to know that sometimes bad things happen to good people.

Because I cannot control the world around me, I try desperately to control what happens within the confines of my own home. The world around me can make me frantic and paranoid, which aren't particularly good traits. I'm such a carefree, glass-half-full kind of person, but even I have moments of doubt and despair sometimes. I know this too shall pass and the feeling will not last forever, but all of this worry is part of life and raising children. Certainly though, not my favorite part. To the credit of humankind and empathy, I find times when there is community worry. That is when I see the best in people. Communities come together and help, there is so much good in the world during tragedy. I believe humans are inherently good, and that gives me hope for our world. No matter what, a perfect day is any day that my four children come safely home to me.

Despite these crazy, unpredictable times, I know that life does go on. Time and time again in our darkest hours, when we feel that the world has stopped moving, we awaken to the march of time. Not on the same course, but just as a matter of movement, we keep going forward. Some days are easier than others, some days are more graceful and certainly more are filled with gratitude than what other days provide, but still the sun rises, the sun sets, and the world keeps spinning, regardless of our individual struggles. It's one of the only things that we can always count on, and in some way, it is comforting to know that when we want to crawl in a black hole never to return, the earth will gently remind us that it is still there waiting for our return. Holding on to even a shred of hope in the most difficult time sometimes only happens through faith. By looking up at the night sky and seeing a star, by watching the waves crash and smelling the salt air, by watching a butterfly roam the garden, sometimes it's that small God's gift that provides us with the only hope we feel that day. And in those times, I am most grateful for them. Grateful that among all the uncertainty, stress and sadness on the other side, there is hope and love. Hope for better tomorrows and love to guide all of us there.

In time, we always seem to find our way back to both hope and love. If we are lucky, we have people around us who will provide the roadmap to get there. They are our tribe, our people, our connecting souls that find their way into our lives that make the darkest of times bearable. I have had them in my own life and have been that person for others. I'm not sure of a lot of things, but what I am most certain of is that family means everything. I was lucky enough to be born into a very large family with a lot of cousins, aunts, uncles, sisters, brothers, grandparents, and family friends. It was always a celebration of love, fun, and happiness. Even when it wasn't a happy occasion, like when we had to get together for funerals. Somehow, we all got through it with love, laughter, and stories of past times.

One of the most important legacies that I would like to leave is the strong bond of my family. Now that I have my own children, and my siblings have their own children and their own lives, I want this tradition of a large close-knit family to continue. I want my family, my children, to be able to experience the same sort of love and happiness that I had the privilege growing up in. Even when the chips are down, and I feel like the world is against me, I know that I can always rely on my family. Can you say that about your own family? If not, start now! It is never too late to embrace your family. Remind them that you love them. They are the ones who will lift you up, but first you have to let them in.

Times have changed so much and so rapidly, and people have become busier and unavailable now more than ever. Somehow, family gatherings have become less and less. We have moved the event down on things we value. Well, there's always tomorrow to begin your traditions. It's the first of the rest of your life, you know. When we consider it an inconvenience to get together or too much of a financial burden, we have misplaced our priorities. But when we gather with family we are whole, we are home; it is our safe haven.

I understand that this may not be the case with everyone, not everybody has had an opportunity like me to win the family lottery, but the point is, it's important to build close relationships with people you value, and prove you value them by spending time together. Family does not have to be a blood relation; it could be close friends from your community, or high school, or college friends. Find that tribe of people that lift you up when you are down. Find the people that make you feel good; the people who inspire you; the people who give sound advice; and have your best interests at heart. Whoever those people are, keep them close to you and celebrate often! Cherish those good friends who will help you grow through this journey called life. Although I do not see my extended family as often as I would like to, we are connected through texts, calls, and other social media. The point is, we keep the bond going, whether in person or not; and when we do get together, so much love is flowing. I am grateful to love them and be loved by them. I want the same for my own children. I want them to feel that same security, that they have a tribe of people who always have their back. One of the reasons why I enjoy the relationship my children have with their cousins, aunts, uncles and grandparents, is because I know how important it is to have a sense of belonging. My kids know that they are part of something beyond our home: and that is their extended family.

Being part of the family is a responsibility as much as it is a blessing. Our children don't want to disappoint us by making poor choices. I know my children will make poor choices; but it's not about punishment. It's about consequences. And that means, it's not always about grounding them or taking away their phone privileges; rather, it's about dealing with the consequences and learning and growing from them. Of course, every day I hope and pray that some of the choices they make will be based on what we have taught them and have shown them through example. As a family, we generally learn together. I remind my children daily how much they are loved and how much they are important to me and to each other. I keep it open, consistent, and constant. Often, I will text Emma a quick one liner throughout the day. Things like, mom loves Emma. Or just a heart emoji whisked off to William. I give them little reminders that I am here for them. For us, it's special and important to communicate with everyone. When it comes to our cell phones, all four of my children are in the Morandi group text, which also includes Peter. Everyone is in the loop when it comes to family-related issues.

My kids are blessed with a close-knit family. There are 12 cousins in all on my side of the family who we lovingly refer to as the Dirty Dozen. My children get to enjoy the connectedness of their cousins, aunts, uncles, and grandparents. Everyone celebrates each other's successes and supports them when they need the help. We are family. In the true sense.

My children learn that their extended family are trusted people who show unconditional love and have helped to shape them emotionally. They are getting to grow up with their cousins and experience all the special events together. From trick or treating, or fireworks or that gigantic turkey on Thanksgiving, there were always reasons to get together.

Wouldn't it make sense to have family trips (and I mean cousins, etc.) to the museums, waterparks, the beach, hiking, camping... you name it. Doesn't it make sense to have your kids playing and getting to know their cousins? The get-togethers build safety, self-confidence, and camaraderie. It's awesome to watch! There are no other people my children would rather be with than family. And for me, that is invaluable. Sunday dinners are becoming a thing of the past, but we still honor this tradition as often as possible. What better example can we show our children of how important family is, than to actually spend time with them. To me, that makes sense.

My children call their grandmother (my mother) to say hello and see if they can get a bite to eat together or catch a movie or even to cut out of school to spend a day in the city together. That is a testament to how important their grandmother is in their lives. They will openly admit that my mother is important to them and tell me how much they love and adore her. Now that my mom has a man in her life (a family friend who I have known for years), my children look at him as a grandfather, and he reciprocates with a lot of love to them. This man is heaven sent (I believe, from my father). He is kind, gentle, takes my kids camping, to the movies, everything a grandfather would do. While he could never replace my own father, he is a wonderful addition to all of our lives. I am honored to have this selfless man in our lives.

The more people I speak with, the more I realize how rare that is now. Having thought long and hard about his, I believe all of this extra stress and overscheduling is a contributing factor to the downfall of family gatherings. Are you too busy to be with your family? I know the hard part is coordinating schedules, but those schedules should revolve around family, not the other way around.

In our family, the 'cousin cult' is a completely insanely unfiltered bunch. You can hear them from miles away. They are rowdy, they are loud, they are obnoxious, and together, they are funny as hell. They are quite a spectacle! The memories, the fun, the love, and the laughter that they all share for each other is something that I hope will always be remembered. My siblings and I had babies all around the same time so the cousins are basically close in age. For many years, about every six months someone was having a baby. In fact, my last child and my sister's last child are fifteen hours apart. They are best friends and it is beyond adorable to watch then grow up together.

At one family gathering, the adults were in another room watching a boxing match. We didn't really think much of it, and the kids didn't seem to be paying attention to what was on TV. At some point, they all went to the basement to play while my sister and I cleaned up after a family dinner. Suddenly we heard some sort of commotion coming from the basement. When we looked closer, all of the cousins were gathered in a circle chanting in unison, "baby fight, baby fight!" There in the middle of the circle stood the two youngest cousins who weren't any older than three. They were both shirtless and wrestling like animals, and the kids were cheering them on.

We weren't sure if we should laugh or be angry. As we managed to get to the middle of this cousin mosh pit, we broke up the baby fight and asked for details. All a mess and sweaty, the kids innocently said, "It's a baby fight, we all took bets on the fight, like you guys did upstairs!" Now, this is the kind of shit you think, *oh, for fuck sake*, these kids don't miss a thing. From that point on, we stopped watching professional boxing around them. Together, they mimicked what they saw.

They made up games, variety shows, and stories and are always there for one another. When you hear "family first" we take that seriously. I value the relationship we have together and am grateful to experience life surrounded with so much love.

No matter the faith, perseverance, or love, parenting is hard. There are no rules, no instructions and no guarantees. My mother always used to say, "You can't put them on a shelf." I never really knew what she meant by that until I had my own children. I didn't realize it at the time, but she was warning us that you can't just have children and think your job is over; that is, they don't just sit on a shelf. It is quite the opposite. They are always in constant motion and change, and there is continuous movement, for there is always work to be done.

I feel that every day is a new adventure which brings new challenges, and my job is to be present, to help navigate this life with them as they are the ones who are in control. The biggest challenge is wanting to be the navigator when I feel the need to take the reins. Sometimes I need to sit and watch them fail, and that is the most heartbreaking action. Some lessons are meant to be learned on their own, without my protection. That's where the growth comes in.

Parents, would you let your kids fail? Are there limits to how much and how far you will let them fail? Are there absolutes about failing? Anyone (which is really **everyone**) who has failed at something will tell you that it sucks to fail. Let it happen anyway. That is the real character builder. I have failed more times than I have succeeded, and all of them made my triumphs more rewarding. I know hard work, discipline, motivation, perseverance, criticism, sadness, joy and success. I know this because I lived it. As much as I want my children to have the happiest of lives, I want them to feel and experience all of the moments, the good and the bad. Through this process they have come to understand my motto, *for fuck sake*. I hope that they appreciate the cold wind, the hot sunshine, the hard work, the reward, the despair, and the hope that life has to offer. This will make them grateful for knowing how to handle the many twists and turns that life will throw at them. My wish is for them to have faith in knowing that there is good in this world and hope in the future. They alone cannot change the world completely, but if we show them how to live with honesty, integrity, and love, they can be part of the goodness of the world.

Chapter 18

Life Will Go on....

When my children were younger I would long for summer. I would wish for it, I would hope the days would pass quickly to get to summer break, I would even count down the days to the last day of school. As they got older, I started to dread it. I truly began dreading each day closer to summer because I knew each summer break meant each fall they would be in one grade higher, which ultimately meant a moment closer to leaving the nest. Although we all want and wish our children to grow older and succeed, every summer is just a little closer to my reminder that they will not be with me, and our family dynamic will change. There are days that my thoughts scare the crap out of me.

It was just yesterday that I was the proud mom of four small children, carting off to crazy places, parading my children as my badge of honor. Raising four kids, just two years apart is like the movie, *Groundhog Day*, except with each kid's unique personality. Talk about a season of living! With each kid we learn a little bit more about parenting, so we adjust for the next kid, then we adjust for next kid, until before you know it, we have four insanely great kids that are growing up way too fast. Now we are talking about college and boyfriends and girlfriends, and their future. Gone are the days of peek-a-boo, and what color cup they want to drink out of. I miss those little faces, with their little problems. The times when a hug and an ice cream cone would make everything better. One thing I was always really good at was appreciating all the stages of their childhood, never rushing the phases of their lives or wishing for another time.

And now, I find myself wishing they were small again, and me being the most important part of their day. Truth be told, to a certain extent I know I am, but now I share them with the outside world. I acknowledge that they have a robust life when away from our home, but I have built a bond with them of trust, communication, and friendship. Don't misunderstand friendship. At the end of the day, I am running the castle and everyone knows it. I am not a lax parent, I am a lot of parent! They know I am a constant in their lives and that I will be there to cheer them up and celebrate them. As most parents are for their children, I am their biggest fan. I want to see them succeed, learn from their failures, and rejoice in all the stuff in between. As they have grown, so have I. I am now a parent to teenagers and I have had to learn to navigate these new waters while still being true to my own journey. Just as the seasons change, so do the seasons of being a mother.

The biggest (and most constant) shift of seasons are the transitions. Going from being completely hands-on during their infancy, to allowing them to explore their surroundings as toddlers, then being away from me during their school age years, and now watching them grow into young adults. Watching them transition into who they are today has been the biggest joy of my life. And now, my teenagers are making independent decisions, and we hope we have taught them to make the right ones.

But what about our seasons? Parenting seasons change as well. We nurture, protect, guide, listen, and observe them as they prepare to become more autonomous. The seasons change, but regardless of what season it may be, one thing we will always do is worry. Worry never stops. If you are reading right now you know exactly what I am talking about. Are they safe? Are they happy? Are they making good choices? *Oh, for fuck sake,* it's exhausting! But it's the kind of feeling that I will never give up.

As the Fab4 keep getting older, I find myself embracing every single moment, not knowing when I will encounter a "last." Last diaper to change. Last baby food jar to buy. Last tooth to fall out, last time holding my hand crossing the street, last time sleeping in my bed because they had a bad dream. Last time they needed my help to go potty. And the list goes on and on. It's like a movie. The *Morandi* movie. I wonder how each day will turn out because every moment, every family dinner, every time we are hanging out in the living room, rooting for the Yankees on TV, and laughing our heads off means the world to me. I know one day my kids will no longer be under my roof doing all these ordinary, everyday things that we generally take for granted. One day, there will be the last one to leave home. I spend a lot of time thinking about it, and maybe I am robbing myself of the present a bit, but I'm also aware of what the future holds. If you were to stop for a minute and think back on your family memories, would they be the same as mine? I ask this question because so many parents are planners for the future. Not the far future for themselves, because that does come in to play until they are older, but the day-to-day shuffling of kids to the baseball games, the band practices, the dentist, the shoe stores, and... what else? We are trained to be future-centered, instead of being in the moment.

The family joke in my house is that I say, "Isn't this nice?" over a lot of very common, mundane, boring situations. My kids will groan when I sing out, "Isn't this nice?" When we are just in the car together, going somewhere, no big deal. And then there's having dinner as a family, or decorating our Christmas tree, or even doing chores around the house together. Positivity, when you are with your children goes a long, long way. You must trust me on this.

The bitter truth is that one day we will not all live under the same roof, or drive in the same car, or regularly have dinner all together, or even rake the leaves all over the front lawn as a family. The truth is, they will grow and leave and have their own families. In so many ways and on so many levels, that terrifies me. I try to wonder what life will be like when all my children are grown with their own families, and there's no one home for Christmas morning, no crazy and beautiful Halloween costumes, no cheering for the tooth fairy, or all the little childhood moments that I get to see through my children's eyes. One day, all of it will just be a memory. Growing up with my children, I have learned to hold on to all of the little stuff: the toothless smiles, the scraped knees, and all their school accomplishments, nor do I forget all the disappointments and struggles they went through.

I wonder, when this is over, who will I be? For one, know I will be a mother who has loved and laughed and cried and worried and loved so profoundly that I cannot find the words to articulate my deep feelings. It just went so darn quick. In a blink of an eye, I watched four babies grow to four children, who will eventually be four adults, who may be parents with children of their own. I can hear myself now: Oh, *for fuck sake*, where did the time go? Well, *for fuck sake*, now what do I do? Oh, *for fuck sake* who am I without being the person who cares for them? Oh, *for fuck sake*, now what? That would be the scary part. I just don't know the answer to any of those things. Yet, my own mother and many mothers before me figured it out. I guess I will as well, but when I look to the future I just can't imagine myself without washing five loads of laundry a day, food shopping, pick-ups and drop offs, all while muttering under my breath, *for fuck sake*. Who am I without them? *For fuck sake,* I do not know yet.

I look in the mirror now, and sometimes I barely recognize the reflection looking back at me. The curves of my body have changed, the shape of my face is older, the new wrinkles on my forehead, laugh lines on my cheeks, and the tiny little wrinkles around my eyes are now blatantly apparent. It seems like yesterday I was young, vibrant, full of tremendous energy, and living my life with my family and believing in endless possibilities. I hold very personal and endearing memories from my childhood, and often I wonder which memories my children will remember. Kids growing up together have real childhood memories that shouldn't include running from place to place and doing things that didn't interest them.

I am now middle aged. In my 20s, I was working hard to build a life with my husband, renovating a home that at the time was just a house. Much of my 20s was not spent at the clubs or partying like so many others my age; instead, Peter and I were building our foundation to what later became our lives today. We knew instinctively that we were good partners for this. We both have the same drive, focus, and desire for a happy, stable home. By the age of 27, I had my first child, William. This changed everything. I decided to take on the role of a stay-at-home mother. That one decision altered the course of my life. Sometimes I wonder where I would be and what I would be doing had I not made a conscious decision be home for my kids.

In my 30s, I continued bearing children practically every two 2 1/2 years. That time was gloriously chaotic. I knew where my children were, I knew they were always safe, and I always knew that we would be together from the minute we wake up until the minute our heads hit the pillow. Every day – joyously watching my children grow. I can remember my younger self, with little children on my lap, vomit on my shoulders, and sleep-deprived eyes. That life was all a second ago, and now the seasons have changed in many profound ways. The days were filled with trips to the museum, indoor picnics, and playground runs. And on those days that we were all home, there were messy afternoons filled with arts and crafts, spilled milk, broken toys, lost Legos, burned Pop tarts, squished grapes, and a whole lot of love. I cherish every precious moment of being with my children, which include the good, the bad, and everything in between.

Now I'm in my 40s and my children are getting older. My son is looking at colleges, my daughter dreams of her high school experience, while my two younger boys are more rambunctious, athletic, and busier than I ever thought possible. And now, every time I look in the mirror I see that reflection of my younger self, in the thick of raising kids. That self that gave everything she had to those four babies; that self that didn't shower for days, never sat for a meal, and always had a weird smell of dried breastmilk and vomit on her shoulder. I wonder, how did I sustain that organized chaos for so many years?

These days, I am a little more selfish than the early years of parenting. Now I know (and so does my family) that I need my seven hours of sleep. I need to eat what I like to eat, and not just mac and cheese. And yes, I like to get dressed up in something other than yoga pants. So, when I look in the mirror and I think oh, *for fuck sake* where has the time gone? When did my breasts start getting so saggy? Where did those wrinkles by my eyes come from? I take a deep breath and think about the memories. Then I laugh out loud, because for the last 20 years I've been on the ride of my life. As I flip through old photos of my younger self as a mom, I focus on my eyes. I stare intently at them, trying to tell if I knew then what the happiest days of my life would look like. Did I know that having my children cuddled up beside me in all of their sweetness would not last forever? Probably not, because I always remember appreciating every moment, every second, every day of being their mother.

There are levels of "gratefulness," and I feel that I have always been grateful by nature. I have always known that nothing is going to last forever, and that one day all the sweet little cuddles, and all the "I love you's" will come to a halt. Next time you look in the mirror, and frown at the wrinkles, the extra weight around your waist, and even the droopiness of things that used to be so perky a time long ago, remember that *for fuck sake,* the reflection looking back at you is a woman who has lived, and loved, and who has had a wonderful journey through life. Even though having a conversation regarding college should be exciting, I find myself longing for my little boy, who insisted we play matchbox cars for just a little longer. Now, as I watch my daughter walk past me while texting on her cell phone, and I make a comment like she looks pretty, she shrugs, smiles, and keeps walking. How I wish we were watching *Dora the Explorer*, and I was brushing her hair again. When I cheered on my baseball player, Benjamin, I would watch him on the baseball field and smile with such pride, especially when he looked over at me to make sure I was watching, and now he barely notices I am there in the stands. My youngest, Matthew, is always ready for a big hug, a hand to be held, and all the *I love you's* are slowly becoming implied, but not said. There was a time that not sleeping in my bed at night was unheard of, and now he kisses me good night, and walks confidently off to his own bedroom where he is snuggled up alone in his own space. I look at these four beings, proud of the people I am raising, but longing for their little bodies, little voices, and their complete dependence on me.

Older kids have ideas and thoughts, and I am always interested in hearing their views. I enjoy having political conversations, engaging in debates over sports and music, and life in general. Hearing the opinions of my children, the perceptions that I helped them form, leaves me proud and unbelievably baffled at their more mature interests and passions. There was a time that William was the one out of the four kids who insisted on matching his blue cup and plate and now he has such strong opinions on climate change.

People always talk about the magic of seeing life through a child's eyes, and although that is amazing, seeing life through a teenager's life is just as magnificent. Teenagers get a bad rap about being sarcastic and self-indulgent, yet they also are witty and interesting and understand life in a different way, and they don't get the credit they deserve. Nothing makes me smile more than my 16-year-old. I know that sounds crazy because most people do not say that about their 16-year-olds. He is happy, friendly, affectionate, and loving toward me. He walks in the door, excited to see me, and his simple words, "Hi mom," makes my entire day. His lack of effort sometimes in school, the missing homework, even his messy room drives me absolutely crazy; but honestly, even with all of that, this child brings me such joy. I feel incredibly fortunate because I know how unusual our relationship is and that it is not typical teenage behavior to be so close to your mother. At some point, there may be drama and heartache, but for now, I'm enjoying this abundance of admiration, and hoping that if the dreaded teenager rears its ugly head, the core of our bond will get us through.

I have wants for all my kids. I want them to grow up to be happy adults, inspiring people, and loving parents. I want them to feel whole even during their struggles. Most of all, I want them to know they are loved, they are treasured, and they have made me learn a love that I never knew existed prior to becoming their parent. I hope that they will look back on their childhood with the same fondness that I hold dear to my heart. I want them to remember the fun- filled days, the laughter, the adventures, but most of all, the abundance of joy that they have brought to my life.

Being a connected mother has always been easy for me, but it leaves little energy and time to be as good a wife as I should. I think the best advice I have ever received about marriage is not to give so much to your children that you have nothing left for each other. The basis of this statement is that your children will grow and the man that is sitting beside you will still be there. I make that mistake a million times and keep trying to get that one right. I'm getting closer, but it's a work in progress and something that I constantly struggle to achieve: finding the correct balance of husband and kids.

Only time will really tell where life will bring any of us, but I do know that I will continue to cherish all the moments, embrace all the love, and enjoy this extraordinary journey of both the *for fuck sakes* and the incredible joy all life has to offer. I just wish this could all slow down a bit, both the good and the bad, so that life can let me hold on a little longer, while I inhale the joys of motherhood, enjoy the challenges and successes of the lives that I brought into this world, and keep me feeling wanted and needed eternally. Even if that is only somewhat true.

Remember my reflection in the mirror and how it has changed over the years? The same goes for when I look at Peter, my husband of 19 years. I notice the lines around his eyes and the gray in his hair. I can see his receding hairline becoming more and more defined. I look at it with a soft smile and admiration. I lived through those wrinkles, and the many gray hairs, and together we are growing old. There's something to be said for that. I feel fortunate that we also got to be young together. We were vibrant, energetic, feisty and determined in those days.

Now, as we have grown older, we have become more patient, peacefully quiet, and prefer the simple things together. A hot cup of coffee early in the morning, a walk before sunrise, a quick getaway to our local pub for a beer, or a bite to eat - just to step away from our schedules and catch up with one another. We both understand that we have a responsibility to our own children to show through our example what a marriage is about. It's not always easy, and we don't always get along; and honestly, we don't always get it right, but the ups and downs, the highs and lows, and our solid partnership is what makes it special. The other night when I was at my sister's house, as I glanced at Peter playing with the youngest in our family, Skylee. She's only five months old and is starting to giggle and has the biggest smile with the cutest dimples you can imagine. As I watched my husband oohhing and ahhing over this little girl, I was drawn to the creases in his face, the wrinkles around his eyes, and the grey in his hair. While he was joyfully playing with this beautiful gift, I imagined that he would one day be a wonderful grandfather. He played with our own children the same way, but at that moment, looking at him in amazement as he was entertained by a five-month-old, made my heart melt.

Sometimes I wonder about what it would be like as we get older, and eventually our own children become parents. It seems like it is so far away. Then someone reminds us, that William is 16 years old already and he could certainly have a child within the next 15 years. Fifteen years? I could be a grandmother 15 years from now? My experience tells me that 15 years is the blink of an eye. I remember 15 years ago as if it happened a moment ago. And now the thought that in 15 years I could be a grandmother. Wow! Life is an amazing journey, and I am in complete awe of how quickly it passes. It is why I feel like I have to hold on to each moment before it's gone. I think this feeling comes from my father dying young. It made me see that growing old is a gift. When I think of my older self, I think of Peter standing next to me. I imagine we will have grandchildren and we will be part of their memories. With the prevalence of social media and the use of my cell phone, we will be the ones taking photos of our grandkids and posting them on Facebook, chronicling every little adorable thing they do. I am sure we will have a lot of "isn't this nice?" moments.

I know my thoughts are premature, because my kids' ages run from 16 down to 9, so I will be doing plenty more parenting for years to come. But sometimes I find myself longing for the days of a pregnant belly, little ones at my feet, and a tremendous amount of baby chaos all around. It seems like a lifetime ago, but it was just a moment. A moment that if I could reach out and grab hold of it, I would never let it go.

Chapter 19

Sometimes You Drop it,
and Sometimes You Rock It

Drop It

SOMETIMES WE LOSE OUR SHIT. SOMETIMES IT COMES OUT OF nowhere. And sometimes it is built up for months and months and months and then finally, you lose your shit! This has happened to me on more than one occasion. One time, some teenagers came to my house drunk and started kicking my fence, demanding that my son come outside for a fistfight. They were just being teenagers trying to start trouble, but once I felt that my son and my home were under attack, I lost my shit. I raced out the front door, bathrobe and all, chasing the kids – all of which were at least two feet taller than me – down the street screaming like a lunatic "Who's the scared one now motherfucker? What? Are you afraid of a middle-aged woman?" Not my brightest moment for sure. Needless to say, my son was mortified. He told me later that he was teased at school for my crazy potty-mouth rant. All I know is that when I am put into a position of fight or flight, my instinct is always to fight. It must be the Italian in me.

I remember another time when I was watching Benjamin's baseball game. Week after week, I would see the same group of kids on the team misbehaving. They weren't paying attention to warnings, and were climbing the fence, ignoring the game, and just causing an overall ruckus. I watched this for about three weeks in a row, when finally, I just couldn't take it anymore. I got up out of my cheap five dollar folding chair, walked over to the dugout, and said, "Listen boys, I have watched you all acting like animals, week after week. You are a distraction to your team, to the other team, to the pitcher, to the catcher, and to everyone watching this game. To see you all behaving so poorly really is such a shame. You are representing your teammates, now sit down on the bench, shut your mouth, watch the game, and maybe learn something about baseball!" I marched off feeling pretty proud of myself – putting those boys in their place. Then I thought, "Oh crap and *for fuck sake,* the other mothers are going to be pretty pissed at me for yelling at their kids." Lucky for me, no one said a thing. Maybe they did so behind my back, but I didn't care. I just could not take watching their disrespect any longer. For the record, I'm not one to lose my shit very easily, or very often. But when you push me to that limit, RUN!

Speaking of times that I've lost my shit, my children are certainly not exempt from it, especially that one particular Christmas Eve. The weeks and days leading up to that night were wonderful. I had been shopping for weeks to make this Christmas extra special. Our usual tradition is to have a house full of people. Neighbors and friends and family stop by, have a drink, and I prepare a nice meal. Santa Claus comes for a visit and even hands out presents for all the children. It's a wonderful and happy tradition, filled with love and joy. It is also a lot of work. I was exhausted from all of the preparation to make the day special. As I was vacuuming, cleaning, preparing, cooking, organizing, setting up, and getting ready for a big Christmas Eve celebration, my four little darlings were always around me or close by and there was nonstop fighting. Bickering, pushing, whining, calling names, teasing, pulling pranks, you name it, it was happening, nonstop. Finally, when I had enough, at the top of my voice I screamed, "Get Out! Get Out! Seriously, get out of the house now." I looked at each kid and they could see that my face was not friendly. "Go! Go! Go outside!" It was freezing cold outside. I gathered all four of them and literally threw them out my front door. No one had socks, shirts, coats, or shoes on, and there they were, huddled up in the corner of the porch. I went back to happily and peacefully doing all of my work, vacuuming and setting up. Like a ton of bricks, it occurred to me that I just threw my four young children out the front door in the freezing cold. When I looked out the front door the four of them were huddled together giggling and poking and teasing and being rowdy, all the while trying to stay warm. When push came to shove, and they were in the situation of banning together, William gave Matthew his sweatshirt and was protecting all of them from the cold. I don't think they will ever forget (or let me forget) the time I threw them out to the front porch on Christmas Eve. It comes up every Christmas and will continue to do so years from now when they tell their children, grandchildren, spouses, and friends. We laugh about it now, but at the time, I surely lost my shit.

Rock It

Now before you call the authorities, these cases are few and far between, and I am mostly calm and cool. For example, Halloween is my most favorite day of the year. Kids all around are excited and genuinely happy and everyone looks forward to the day. There are celebrations at schools, parades, trick-or-treating, and plenty of parties to go around. I love seeing all the little kids dressed up in their costumes, with big smiles and anticipation of what candy is going to be collected during the day. My favorite kids are the ones where their parents put in so much time and effort and make their costumes. I salute you, Parents! The uniqueness, time and creativity that goes into these costumes completely amaze me. Especially the families who all have the same-themed costumes. I approach every October with great intentions, but every year, I find myself at my local party store staring up at a board filled with various costumes paying no less than 40 dollars a costume for whatever the popular character is of that year. So that's four kids, times forty dollars. That equals $160 for an evening of crazy fun that involves candy. So, every year I flip through the Pier One catalog with the intention of replicating the adorable Halloween oasis scene on the pages, and every year I fail miserably. I thumb through the pages, I have a game plan, I am ready and willing to shell out an exorbitant amount of cash for cheap holiday decorations. Then I get to the store and reality sets in. The cost of going all out for Halloween is far more expensive than I am willing to spend, so I end up walking out with a stupid scarecrow and change in my pocket. It's a cycle, and at this point, my kids have completely called me out on it. I come home with "bargain" decorations and they always ask, "Why didn't you buy the big blow- up pumpkin? I thought you were going to get the good spider webs this year!"

I know. I know, kids. Maybe next year.

When my children were younger, every year I would try to make Halloween absolutely perfect for them. Get them the best costumes, decorate the house, have big parties, but in the process, I always become filled with such anxiety because I wanted to pull off the very perfect holiday for them. As they got older and wanted to be with their friends it tugged at my heart strings a bit. In all selfishness I wondered, "Why don't you want to be with us?" That's the pulling away I mentioned earlier. Those are the changes that tug at my heart. Even so, I still make the same effort and treasure Halloween like I did when they were little. I am still making sure to have the best candy selection, special treats for them when they wake up, taking pictures, and always being as genuinely and equally excited for their favorite holiday. Hours and hours walking the streets with them trick-or-treating, watching them go from door-to-door, running as fast as they could to see how much candy they could get in just one afternoon. Without fail, every Halloween, one of them eats too much candy and gets sick. None of them ever considers the sugar rushing to their heads, the stomach turning and churning, and the feeling like they might throw up, and thought that maybe they should slow down on the candy consumption. Nope, not my kids. They will eat and eat and eat every delicious morsel of that candy until they are covered with wrappers that are littered around them and they have a bellyache. Here's where I am the Halloween Hero. I'm the kind of mother who will let my kids eat candy from the moment they wake up to the time they are holding their stomach with regret. Sticky faces, hands, and clothes on Halloween is just proof that it was another epic event. I am also a real champ when it comes to trick or treating. Regardless of the weather, regardless of how tired I am, or how many houses we go to, I will not stop trick-or-treating until the kids tell me they want to go home. I can be freezing, utterly exhausted with blisters, while carrying pounds of candy through the neighborhood, I simply will not complain. Well, I mean no complaints pass my lips. In my mind, I'm thinking, *for fuck sake,* how much candy can one 60-pound child eat? I act excited by all the sticky little treats that will inevitably be left on the floor for the dog to get, and then suffer from diarrhea. I never make a set time as to how long we will be out, or ever complain going door-to-door to the houses of complete strangers for free candy. I'm all in on Halloween, no questions asked, no verbal complaints. Although as we walk through the neighborhood, I think *for fuck sake,* we have about 10 pounds of candy, we're surely going to rot our teeth and get diabetes by the end of this day. I keep my worries to myself, and a smile on my face for every Babe Ruth they score. Yes, Halloween is a joyous occasion that I will forever hold close to my heart. It is one that I cherish more than any other holiday of the year because it is the one day the kids can act like complete lunatics and are disguised so people can't tell they are mine.

With each passing Halloween, I know the spirit is lost just a little bit, but as long as you give my kids free candy, the excitement and joy of the day will always be the best day of the year for them. Of course, the next day is a different story. No one wants to go to school and everyone is feeling yucky. They give me reasons why it's a bad idea to go to school: no one's going to be there; it's a Catholic holiday; I'm a saint and it's all Saints Day; I need the day off; they're having a major field trip, and no one will even be there. It never ceases to amaze me that each year they downright demand they should stay home and every single year I downright demand that they go to school, "No way, no how, not in this universe." They mumble and moan, but eventually they get out the door. Later in the day when I ask how many kids were in class, the universal answer is no one. "No one?" I ask. Adamantly, they reply, "no one." I know it's not true. Every mother I know sends her child to school on all Saints Day. After all, *for fuck sake,* we parents *are* the saints.

Drop It (Literally)

I'm a pretty competitive girl. Maybe it's because of this nature that I did well with running. Truth be told, I hate to lose. When I am on your team you can bet that I am bringing my A game. I will do what I need to do to help lead my team to victory. When Emma was a baby I was involved with a not-so-friendly family whiffle ball game. She was at the age where she was clingy and wouldn't let me put her down for long. At this point, the score was tied and it was my turn up to bat. Here I am, holding Emma, straddled on my left hip, wondering, do I make her cry and bat, or do I sit out of the game and run the risk of losing? The quick thinker I was, I did what any rational competitive mother would do, I held her and batted at the same time. That made perfect sense. First ball thrown, strike and a miss, this multitasking was going to be more difficult than I anticipated. Second ball thrown, a foul, okay... okay, I got this. Next, with Emma in one arm and the bat in the other, the ball comes at me and I swing and a hit! I was so excited that I hit the ball, I dropped Emma on the ground, and off I went running toward first base. As I was celebrating my victory I look down at my baby crying on the grass as the other players (who were my family members) froze, just staring and stunned at me, confused at my decision to drop my baby on the ground to win the game. Of course, I felt terrible afterward, and to this day none of them let me live it down. I do remember that the celebration of the win and drinking that cold beer, made it all worth it. Well, not really. I still kind of feel badly about it. What I learned from that experience is that sometimes I can get carried away. I get lost in the moment of feeling victory that I forget what's important, like my baby on the grass that I dropped in the middle of a family whiffle ball game.

Rock It

With all the incredible joy that motherhood may bring, there are certain downfalls to the job. For one, your body will never quite be the same. Since having my fourth child I've had uncontrollable and embarrassing bladder problems. It's a good thing I have such a great sense of humor because peeing my pants has become a common daily occurrence in my life. Now, I am not talking about a little tinkle or a little wet spot, I am talking about a full blown urinated mess. It's downright brutal at times. The sensation comes out of nowhere. One moment I'm driving in my car, and the next I know I'm panicking, searching desperately for a restroom, a bush, or even a place where someone cannot see what is about to take place. My friends all know this about me and everyone just accepts it. I actually joke that I can be professional pee-er. Is that actually a job or a word? I'm not sure. But if it is, I'm your girl. I can literally urinate anywhere. Most times I will be urinating in a public place and not one person will even know what's going on. Yes, I'm that good. One time I was at the beach and I knew I would never make it all the way up the beach to the restroom. I had a choice: pee my pants, go into the frigid water, or be a little innovative. I decided to figure out a way that did not involve me getting wet from the ocean or my pee. I put a beach blanket around me and did my business. If you think I wear it as a badge of honor, you are right! Listen, if you're going to have an embarrassing situation, you might as well be good at it. I turned a *for fuck sake* situation into a triumph. And I think there's something to be learned from that. There are things that happen in our lives that we can't always control, we can live in shame or embarrassment, or we can hold our heads up high and say *for fuck sake*, I'll make the best of it.

Drop It

You know the women who are always stylin'? The beautiful ladies with matching earrings, purses, accessories, and shoes. Yeah, I'm not one of them. Even when I do manage to make myself look halfway decent, I feel so out of place, like I'm dressed up in my mother's clothing. I'm just the kind of gal who feels happier and prettier when I am dressed down. Boy, but I do love admiring these ladies and all their elegance, as they strut with their high heels and perfectly matched clothing, and I think, "One day... one day I'll try to be that girl." I know damn well that will never happen, but a girl can dream.

I prefer loose fitting, comfortable, more casual clothes. When I was a kid, I loved penny loafers and big sweaters, so this is not something new for me. Nowadays, my favorite outfits are Target brand sundresses, and I like to dress it up with a scarf. In the summer, you could almost be assured I will be in a dress, with flip-flops on, and my hair in ponytails. But when the cold weather hits I'm almost always at a loss as to what to wear. If I'm really in a sassy mood, I'll even throw on some jeans, a pair of earrings, and a nice sweater. More likely than not, I am in sweatpants, anxiously waiting for the clock to tick to that glorious time when it is socially acceptable to put on my pajamas. At the end of the day, pajamas are my all-time favorite clothing attire. It is a special feeling for me; I am completely at ease, inside and out. There's nothing more comforting than knowing that I have some soft cotton pjs waiting for me to get to my happy place.

Rock It

I have always been a good saver. A saver of money, as well as a saver of memories. My husband often teases me, calling me a squirrel because I am always finding a way to "squirrel away" a little extra cash. Whether it be collecting empty water bottles, to saving all loose change in a jar, and then depositing it into a secret fund to be used at a later date, saving money for me is important because it provides a security for any *fucks sake* moments. There are plenty of times when there was an *oh, for fuck sake*, the washer just died, or *for fuck sake*, we have a leak in the bathroom, *oh for fuck sake*, one of the kids outgrew all of their clothes again, and there I am, prepared for it because of the money I squirrelled away. I don't mind being teased for it, and I take a certain amount of pride to be able to have these meager savings for small emergencies. Besides, it also shows my children how to prepare for real life mishaps by taking small steps. It may not be glamorous to return bottles or cash in change, but glamorous does not always equal success. Success comes from small steps, preparation, and the willingness to skip the glitz and glamor.

Just as important, I am a saver of memories. I document just about everything. I have journals of everything dating back from before I was married. I love to be able to look back and have a record of the days of the younger me in college with so many hopes and dreams, meeting Peter and not knowing at the time that he would one day be my husband, the unexpected engagement proposal, the excitement of my wedding day, the sadness of the various deaths that I have endured, the births of my children, the milestones of my life and all of the in-between moments. Sometimes I look through these old journals and smile with so much love about those times, and sometimes I get a little melancholy about how those times seem to be a lifetime ago, yet just a moment away. It's a strange experience, but I am so grateful to have them all. I'm the same way with pictures, I have every month of my children's life documented with pictures, from the first time eating baby food, rolling over, walking, and birthdays, to the first day of school, first time roller skating, and even that first kiss! Trust me, it takes a lot of work to keep all the memories organized, but it is definitely worth doing. These amazing books of memories are filled with stories of our lives together, and precious moments shared.

Saving memories and cherishing times are when I am at my best. Celebrating birthdays to me are very special. I make a big deal out of them. For the kids, the celebration of their birth begins with a birthday breakfast, balloons, presents and my personal sheer joy in getting to celebrate their life. I try to spend time alone with each child on their birthday to celebrate the special bond between mother and child. Every year Emma and I spend the day together, and then go to dinner with the boys. We always find something to do, usually lunch, nails, horseback riding, movies, or anything we can think of. It's kind of a tradition at this point. For as long as she will allow me, is as long as I will allow her to take the day off from school and spend her birthday with me. I realize eventually she will have her own family and her own life, and probably will be spending her birthday with others. But for now, I absolutely treasure each birthday that I get to spend with my little girl.

And Sometimes, There Is A Compromise

I am a rock star when it comes to time management. Peter has told me that I am the most efficient person he knows. Now, either he hangs around people with no time management skills or I'm really that good. I like to believe it's my rock-solid, schedule savvy, get-it-done, way of life. Every moment of my day is accounted for, not a second to waste. From the moment my feet hit the floor in the morning, I'm on the go. No time to sit for a cup of coffee when there's laundry to be done, beds to be made, and errands to be run almost immediately upon waking. I like to keep my house in order, my laundry loads at a minimum, and my refrigerator stocked with food. But all of that takes time. It takes time management. It takes scheduling. And so I don't have a lot of time to waste. I am the ultimate multitasker. Like most women, I don't just do one thing at a time. Peter and I constantly disagree about this. According to his calculations, it is ultimately impossible to do more than one thing at a time. I call fiddle-faddle on that one. I'm doing at least three to five things at a time and I'm doing them well. It frustrates him to see me not concentrating on one thing at a time, and he is not shy to remind me of it. For me, one task at a time seems crazy. I would never get everything done in a timely, efficient manner. I bite my tongue when I see how much slower he moves than me; I have to refrain from screaming to hurry up, we have four kids and a whole lotta shit to do today! Although not perfect, I do try to keep my thoughts to myself, after all we are different people and work at a different pace and do things in a different capacity. I could never fix anything in this house, including changing a lightbulb. In my home Peter is far more organized, and much handier than I could ever hope to be. He knows when to change air filters and when the smoke alarms need new batteries. He keeps us safe.

A perfect example of how Peter and I work differently is when we are coming at two different directions for a collaborative project. Here is an example of what I mean. We had a scheduled meeting with a financial advisor and needed to fill out a pile of paperwork within two weeks' time. Of course, we waited for the last couple of days to even review what documents we would need for the meeting and were in panic mode to complete this daunting task of filling out the large amount of forms, which included going through many records, making calculations, and organizing our thoughts for the meeting. At the end of a very busy weekend, Peter was completely irritated and exhausted by the thought of sitting down to do this. I wanted to discuss it over an early dinner with the forms nearby so that I could fill them out while we were eating. Peter, on the other hand, wanted to first finish the meal, clean up the kitchen, and then work on the papers. To me, that made no sense at all. I couldn't even fathom the thought of wasting time by putting it off until after dinner. There was a lot of paperwork to be done, the kids were out of the house, and it was the perfect opportunity to quickly eat and work and get the task done efficiently and effectively. Besides, that was an important night. You see, I am a diehard New York Yankees fan and it was Game 7 of the World Series against the Arizona Diamondbacks. We both knew what that meant, and the last thing either one of us wanted to do was miss that game. The only solution to making that happen was do the damn paperwork while we ate. Make sense? Meanwhile, Peter was aggravated that I wouldn't sit and enjoy a meal first, and then dive in to all that paperwork. A perfectly linear thing to say: eat, then work. The fact is, my husband enjoys experiences, while I enjoy results. Which brings me back to multi-tasking. Let's get it done now. The fact is, we think differently when it comes to those situations. One is not more right or more wrong than the other, it is just different, and in marriage it is all about compromise. But back to that night. We both agreed that *for fuck sake,* let's fill out the paperwork and watch the game together.

With all the **rock it** and **drop it** moments, you come to realize that this thing called life will always be a constant shift. Perhaps like me, you try to be one way, soon realizing that it is not your natural or comfortable self. It's not too late to turn the page and begin a new story. I am a firm believer in living, learning, making mistakes, and growing. Maybe you've come to the point where you are wanting a change. You may want to pull your family in and spend time with everyone as a family unit. Teach them to love and respect their siblings and laugh with them along the way. Every day you get a chance to try again. Is tomorrow your day?

Now, *for fuck sake,* listen closely. You can craft your story from this point on, you can make what you want out of motherhood with all its glory and all its struggles, and certainly with all it's *for fuck sake* moments. This is your art, this is your canvas, and you can drive it and make it any way you choose. Some of us are more patient, more kind, more athletic, more creative, more intellectual, more organized, more fun, and more... (fill in the blank). This is our story, our own personal journey, and although our books may be written a little differently, we are all in this together.

I want to share this story with you. I know this one mom that every time I drop off her child during my turn for carpooling, I see that her front porch is always thematically (and impeccably) decorated for every imaginable holiday. From Groundhog Day to Christmas to Halloween to Easter. You name it, she's got it. Her beautifully put-together daughter explains how her mother does cool arts and crafts with her and makes all sorts of amazing treats for when she gets home. I'm fascinated by this woman. I love that about a fellow mom, but that's just not me. I cannot force myself to be artsy, just like another mother could not force herself to be carefree. We each come into motherhood with our own strengths and weaknesses. Embrace your "**drop it**" along with your "**rock it**" moments. All the experience, knowledge and love you bring to your children, are the things that make up your personal life story. Live it, love it, and encompass the perfectly imperfect being that you are.

Chapter 20

Know your limits

In my own life I try to be the bigger person. When people are rude, I show kindness. When people are gossiping, I show integrity. When people are judging, I show open mindfulness. I cannot control the actions of those around me, but I can control my own actions. I strive to hold myself to a higher standard. I lead by example, I am friendly, kind, and truthful. In a world where we can get caught up in fitting in and lowering our standards, I try to always set the bar high, and be who God has intended me to be. The word *integrity* is one of the most important words in the English language. To me, integrity means everything: Integrity with my actions, integrity with my words, integrity with my motivation, and integrity with my thoughts. Having integrity is not as easy as it sounds, but for me it is always worth it. Staying true, speaking my truth, and living my truth has been one of the greatest life lessons. Teaching my own children to do the same has been both a struggle and a blessing. I have learned from living this truth that it comes with a price. Here's how: I'm always surprised about what strong opinions my kids have about things that are none of their business. From vacations, to house projects, to cars purchases, and even the outfits I wear. Whereas, when I was a kid, I do not remember a time when I was involved in adult decisions. Whatever my parents decided, I knew never to inject my opinion. In fact, I would never dare to even make an expression either way about any adult conversation, nonetheless share my thoughts. But not my kids. They reject wall coloring, vacation routes, and even hairstyles. When did they get the power? Who gave them the power? And *for fuck sake* how the hell do I get it back? But then I realize, we gave them the power, by listening and valuing their opinions and thoughts. Truth be told, I do like to hear their opinions without limits. It gives them a voice in our home and teaches them that their opinions matter. Here is the catch. I like to listen to their reasoning and then ultimately, I get to make the final decision. In our home we have something called The Pineapple. The Pineapple comes up when we say NO to whatever hair brained scheme that they conjure up and then they can call a "Pineapple." I have no idea why or where this name came from, but it did, and it stuck. I then give them the opportunity to express their case and give reasons why my no should become a yes. This gives them the opportunity to articulate their wants and feel that they have been heard. At the end of the conversation I make the final decision, but it's always entertaining to hear some of the stuff they come up with. The practice of negotiating will later be beneficial in their lives. Admittedly, we are "progressive" parents, but *for fuck sake,* all this listening is all so exhausting, yet I wouldn't change a thing. Some may argue that the "Pineapple" is ridiculous and not very 1970's at all. But it's all in your perspective now, isn't it?

Perspective. What a funny thing. Perspective is often confused with reality or truth. One's perspective does not necessarily mean the truth, it is simply that person's truth. I try to keep this in mind when my kids come home with stories and situations, as told from their perspective. If I were one to take their version of their truth at face value, I would think every teacher was unfair, every child was a bully, every coach was too competitive, and every homework assignment too much. But I don't because I realize that their version of the truth is merely their perspective of that situation. If we were to take ten parents, put them in a room and had them say out loud their child's perspective of the same event, there would be ten different stories. For that reason, I am always careful to ask questions, and help my children see things from another's perspective (there's that word again.) Here is a great example: Tweens, especially girls, are full of constant drama. In one particular case, two set of Emma's friends were fighting over something as trivial as where to sit in the lunch room. Emma thought she was doing the right thing by approaching one group of friends to explain their point of view, and then did the same toward the other group. By the end of the day, both groups of friends were mad at Emma and she came home in tears. In her mind, she was trying to bring everyone together. But through the eyes of her friends, she was gossiping to both groups about the other. Perspective. Hard lessons to learn, but so very important. If the meaning of this word is not taught to your kids, they will grow up thinking that their perspective is the only perspective. That's where the "Pineapple" comes in handy. They know they are being heard and, in turn, will learn the art of listening, appreciating, and respecting others' perspective as well.

On countless occasions, I have uttered the words *are you fucking kidding me?* In these instances, I am more baffled than usual. Our generation of parenting is struck with a different set of challenges than past generations. We now are competing with social media, smart phones, video games, and more online distractions than ever before. Watching people on YouTube is far more entertaining and addictive than any of us initially realized. All of these social media forums mean the world to my kids. It is their understanding and connection to the world. How do you respect the culture of this generation while still holding strong to your belief of raising children in a simpler fashion? We can limit the use or take away the phone, but that is just a band aid. The bigger picture is teaching children that being present in the now is more important than their commitment to their online "friends." For my family, this has been a hard sell. Generations before us did not have this challenge, we have entered a new territory. I'll admit, if I knew what I know now and the consequences that would lie before me, I would not have been so easily persuaded to allow all this technology into our home.

When we were kids and it was time for practice or a game, we would happily have hopped into the car and were ecstatic to leave the house. I would look forward to practice so that I could get out of the house to see my friends. Now it is an entirely different experience. Kids are distracted by electronics, online friends, video games, music videos, and all sorts of other devices. So now we are busier with a stronger commitment to extra-curricular activities while trying to get them off the electronics long enough to be prepared. It's exhausting. It's during those times that I say, *are you fucking kidding me?*

To capture your child's attention, and to keep it, is more difficult than ever before. How do we stay calm in these situations? I'm not entirely sure. What I have learned to do is set the expectation of when we are leaving and what they need. If they aren't ready, I simply say - let me know when you are ready. By refusing to engage in their lack of preparation, they know that I won't tolerate tardiness. My point is well taken and they understand the timeframe and the limits. No yelling.

Okay. Let me tell you something I have been holding back throughout this book. My husband and children have it made. They wake up every morning to homemade smoothies, lunch is freshly made, the home is always clean, errands are always run, and generally I always have a smile on my face. I also know that I live a very blessed life and am able to financially, physically, and emotionally care for them. I don't take staying home lightly. I take my job as a mom and wife seriously, consistently making sure my family comes first, the house comes first, their needs before mine. Even with the best intentions, I can't always make everyone happy all of the time. The age-old debate about parents who stay home with their children vs work outside of the home is one that I think about often. I don't know what is the "better" choice for others, but all I do know is what is good for my family. Having me home is what's good for them. Like any job, I am not always going to get it right. The complaints that I didn't get the right orange juice or the correct cereal, I would imagine are easier than the boss who complains about late deadlines or bad business deals. My goal is to teach my children that whatever job they have, they must do it well. It builds character, it shows integrity, and all the small efforts are what will shape them into the adults they will become. My kids know that all the everyday decisions, from making your bed in the morning to preparing for a test in the evening, are the little things that make up your character. These tasks show discipline and preparation. Living a compassionate life means that you take the time out of your day to lend an ear, lend a hand, or lend your time. Those small character builders eventually make up a well-rounded, compassionate person. Same thing goes for so many other character traits. If you want to be athletic, you must participate in sports. That requires practice, being on a team, learning teamwork, knowing how to take orders from a coach, and so on. All those little steps that you help to prepare your children for may seem minor, but in reality, we are helping to build their character. When I'm tempted to say, oh it doesn't really matter much, I stop myself and realize that the small things that you do, actually do matter. After all, the small steps become the bigger steps, and the bigger steps become who your children will be. It may not seem like a big deal when they forget to take out the garbage, clean their room, don't do well in school, or aren't home in time for curfew, but it does mean something; it's called character building. My job as a parent is to raise responsible, caring, happy, successful human beings. And all these little things along the way is what's going to get them there. Admittedly, I'm not the strictest parent, but I do believe in certain principles. I believe in kindness, I believe in taking responsibility, I believe in respect, and I believe in making mistakes. Throughout every day of raising children, I am faced with all the little things that somehow mold them into the people that I am putting out into the world. When one of my children forgets to take out the garbage, or doesn't complete his or her homework, or is unkind to a sibling, I need to correct that behavior. It doesn't necessarily mean that I'm going to punish them where it's going to be some big dramatic situation, but there needs to be a correction. If I don't teach them, who will? I make mistakes every day, and my kids make mistakes every day, if I don't show them how to right the wrong they will never learn.

It sounds silly, but I always park far from the store that we go into. And I always put back my cart after I'm finished shopping. My kids make fun of me for it and constantly complain about it, but I continue to do it. Why? For one, parking farther away gives me a little bit more exercise, I am healthy and able to walk the few extra steps that others may not be able to do. Also, it allows others to park closer to the store that actually need it, by freeing up closer parking spots. Maybe there is someone who has a headache or a cold or is pregnant or not feeling well or just broke a leg or is handicapped or elderly who may need a closer parking spot more than I do. Indirectly, I'm teaching my children to think of others. By putting my shopping cart away, I teach them responsibility. I took the shopping cart out of the store and it is my responsibility to return it to its appropriate location. It would be very easy for me just to leave it next to my car and find the closest parking spot, but it's not necessarily the right thing to do. I consistently do the small deeds and hope that they are picking up on my actions. The little things lead to bigger things. Even when my children were much younger, I always parked farther away and made them walk through the parking lot to the store. They would whine and complain the entire time, but I would remind them that we are actually saving time by not going around in circles searching for the perfect parking spot. But the bigger lessons to invoke were not to be lazy and pay attention to your surroundings when you are in a parking lot. Don't look for the easy way, there are no shortcuts, and hold yourself to a higher standard. One thing for sure, I am not lazy. I hate lazy. I don't like for my children to act lazy, basically because I don't want them to grow up to be lazy adults. My father used to say, "If you don't have time to do it right the first time, how will you find the time to do it right the second time?" I find myself saying that to my own children now. Just do it. Get it done. Having that can-do attitude will get you so much farther than you think. When my kids are complaining about a project that may be due, or too much homework, or an extra chore I might have given them, I simply demand, "Go get it done, it's taking you longer to complain about it than to just do it!" In my mind, I'm saying *for fuck sake,* stop whining and go get it done. Of course, I edit my words and make it sound nicer out loud than it does in my head.

I have never been one to put something off until tomorrow, I don't live that way. I can't prescribe to that mentality. Maybe it's because my father died young and I know far too well that tomorrow is never promised. Therefore, I never wait until the next day. If it's on my list, I want it done today. Life is short, I like to live every day like it's my last. I must admit, however, that this mindset has also been one of my biggest downfalls. I over-book, over-stress, and I am in a constant state of being overly-frantic. It's a balance that I have not yet mastered, but that is one of the benefits of living in a perfectly imperfect mindset. I continue to struggle with balance and know that practice makes perfect. Regardless, I find and use every moment of my day to be the best me that I can be. I sometimes take that theory to the extreme. Putting others ahead of myself, didn't always work out well. I think back on those times that I put others' needs in front of my own without any worry, and now I realize that being selfless can also be foolish.

Back in 2007, when I was eight months pregnant, I took a vacation. As the plane landed and I stood up, I remember holding my belly and literally looking in between my legs, hoping my water didn't break. I remember casually thinking, "Super, I didn't give birth and now I won't ruin everyone's vacation." My sisters and brother and mom decided to take a trip to the Dominican Republic as an effort to heal from our father's death. My family was in turmoil, there was so much anger, sadness and stress after he died, that we thought coming together would help bring a little brightness into a very dark time. I knew I wasn't supposed to be traveling, especially overseas, but I felt that this vacation could be the happiness all of us needed in an otherwise dark time. I already had a lot of issues with my pregnancy, but it was such a crazy time that I carelessly decided to leave the country. I took the four and half hour international flight, both very pregnant and very grateful to be surrounded by my family, with hopes that all would go well.

I read that one of the dangers of flying while pregnant is that the landing may cause women to go into labor. As we prepared to land, I held onto my belly and prayed all would be okay. As it turned out, I didn't give birth at all, and it would be another month and two weeks before my baby arrived. All the while in the Dominican Republic I was such a good sport, wobbling around with everyone at 8 1/2 months pregnant and enjoying all the moments with my family. Most people would know their limits and choose not to put themselves in difficult situations. I, on the other hand, felt the need to join them because they wanted all of us to be together, like we were that last night when we washed my father as he lay dying in his hospital bed. I don't think many expectant moms would take the trip when they are so close to giving birth. My family wanted me there and I didn't hesitate. As it turned out, we all had a positive experience, but I'm thinking that the person I am today would have put more thought in my decision to go, than risking my health.

It's always been this way for me, a day and a half before giving birth to my first child, I was in New York City apartment shopping with my college-age sister, while my father lay in a hospital bed and my mother by his side. I have always taken on the responsibility of my youngest sister's keeper. Back in 2002, it was no different. We drove to New York City in her beat up, no air-conditioned car on literally the hottest day of the summer. Then we walked for miles, looking at different apartment buildings to get her settled for the September semester. It's no surprise that I went into labor two weeks early with my first born.

Again, with my daughter in 2004, on her due date I was babysitting my niece and took both William and his cousin Anelie, both 2 ½, to see a movie and get lunch at the mall. On my due date, I am again wobbling around a mall, with two 2 ½ year olds. Do you see the pattern? Always going, going, going - making everyone else happy without thinking of my own consequences. Sometimes it's a great treat, other times I spread myself so thin and then begin to feel resentful. In any case, in the past decade I have learned to love me enough to know my own limits and to value myself before others. Because of my learning disability as a child, I grew up with an internal feeling of being a burden, which in turn made for an overly helpful, abundantly self -sacrificing adult. I work hard to change that pattern that does not serve me well. Truth be told, it has been a learning process, one I struggle with on a regular basis.

Recently, someone close to me said that I have become more selfish. It wasn't meant as an insult or disparaging in any way; it was a compliment of how far my self-love has grown. In the past, I found myself in many instances, saying *for fuck sake,* does anyone care how thin I am spreading myself? What I should have been asking is *for fuck sake,* Donna, why are you allowing this? You make the rules you set the boundaries, you are in charge of you. For many years, I was the master of yes to others and no to myself. When I finally gained the confidence, maturity, and frankly, the balls to say no, it was empowering. Now when I say yes, it's because I want to say yes, and in the end, all the no's lead me to the most valuable yeses.

Chapter 21

Embrace the Journey

IT'S A COOL CRISP DAY AND AS I WATCH THE LEAVES CHANGE colors on the trees and fall to the ground, I remember all the leaf piles that my kids raked together throughout the years. In my own mind, I can see them jumping in the piles of newly gathered leaves and throwing them effortlessly and carefree. May all the days and their innocence stay with them through their lives.

As we grow older we become more guarded and, quite frankly, less fun. I hope that the child within them will always stay in their soul. There is a child in all of us, waiting for the adult inside to let that inner child seep through to our everyday life. I wish more people would allow for that more often. After all, life is just a series of seasons with constant change and constant growth. One favorite lesson that I have learned being married to Peter is that anything is possible, nothing needs to stay the same, and you can constantly be reborn if you allow yourself to do it. Even though I never had a traditional career, when I started out I went to school for law, worked as a contract negotiator, worked in a talent agency, worked in media, was a stay at home mom, a running coach, a health coach, and to this day, I continue to explore my talents. While those small journeys through my life have led me to this point now, each one was a season of learning and growing.

In my soul, I always wanted to be a writer. From a very young age, I knew that this was the path for me. I was too afraid to listen to that voice deep down inside of me until now. Although I wish I had the courage to pursue this long ago, it just wasn't my time. I didn't have the confidence or the life experience to make me go for it. I mention this because I hope that my children will follow their passions and their paths on their own terms, in their own way, and at their own time. It took me a long time to believe that I was smart enough, courageous enough, and talented enough to do this. I hope my kids find their voice sooner than I did. I also hope that I have shown them through my example how to live a joyful journey with integrity, kindness, and a love for life. In a society where we are judged on looks, wealth, and prestige I want my kids to strive for kindness, compassion, and love. I know that they will be successful if they continually stay true to themselves. Being raised with two ambitious, determined, and hard-working parents, we have laid the groundwork for them to follow in the path of success. I am sure there will be many bumps and roadblocks along the way, but I want them to keep faith that all the bad breaks they may experience will be rewarded with good ones.

What I know to be true is that in our children's life time, there are going to be hard times, times of despair and sadness, and even complete devastation. There will be times of uncertainty, confusion, and internal conflict. And times where they feel so alone and abandoned. The years raising children will be years filled with so many emotions, growth, and memories. Not all of them will be good. There have been times in my life that I thought would last forever and other times that I hoped would last forever, and then there were times where I wish I could just forget. The important part of these times is that they are all just a season.

Through all the work, the hard times, and the struggle of this adventure of raising children, it is important to be able to have self-reflection. Reflecting and thinking freely allows us to stop and take inventory of our own actions, motivations, and thoughts on any situation. Self-reflection has made me more aware of how I handle certain situations and what I could do differently next time. Unfortunately, most people don't take the time or think they have the time to self-reflect. It's just all part of that chaotic life that we have created for ourselves that make us miss out on so many important lessons that will help us tomorrow and be more positive and calm today. Often times we bury ourselves in work, mindless television, alcohol, or just stupid stuff, just to avoid taking the time to self-reflect. Although it may be easier to stay at the office, to have an extra glass of wine, or watch silly videos on YouTube, I think we could all benefit from a little quiet time inside our own minds. My truest hope is, if nothing else, this book has provoked you to dig deep and re-evaluate your own time as a parent.

I remember when my kids were young, and we were leaving Jones Beach State Park in Wantagh, New York. We just came from the playground where they were catching frogs and playing so freely and were so happy and content. At that moment I remember thinking how I wish they would always feel this at peace with their lives. I also wanted them to realize something else, something bigger. While we were walking to our car from the boardwalk, I told them to look out to the ocean to see how beautiful it is here on Long Island. I knew they didn't know what I meant, but I asked them if they realized how fortunate they were to live on Long Island. I also wanted them to know that there's a great big world out there, with so much to see, so much to do, and so much opportunity. Kids think that the world revolves around them and the comfort of their small town, but there's so much more to discover. Kids sometimes don't realize how big the world is, and they get stuck in the now, in the what-if's, in the brand-name clothing, and in what people think. What they don't realize is their immediate experience is just a blip on their map of life. It's a hard concept for kids to realize that no one will remember or care about all the little incidentals that happened in grade school, middle school, and even high school, it's about the bigger picture. I wish more people would understand that - including parents. All these little stresses are just helping to form the future generation, but all the small stuff does not define our kids, it shapes them.

If you were to write a job description about being a parent, no sane person would apply for it. It would read something like this: lack of sleep, constant worry, consistent sacrifice, nonstop conflict, guilt, arranging numerous schedules, solving constant social, emotional and physical ailments, with the benefit of absolutely zero gratitude, zero pay, and zero acknowledgment. I mean, what rational human being would ever take that job? What if I were to tell you it also comes with an abundance of love, satisfaction, humility, pride, and an understanding of life and love that you never knew existed? All of these things are true. Parenting is both conflict and solution, both worry and peace, both struggle and resolution, both humility and pride, but most of all parenting is love. A love cannot be taught, a sacrifice that you don't mind, a pride that cannot be replicated, and a devotion that cannot be explained. With absolute certainty, I can assure you that the following *for fuck sake* is going to happen. *For fuck sake,* as soon as you wash the floors, someone is going to spill orange juice. *For fuck sake,* as soon as you wash all the bedroom sheets, someone's going to wet the bed. *For fuck sake,* if you have plans for tomorrow, someone is going to get a fever. *For fuck sake,* someone is going to get a failing grade, a missed homework, and perhaps even detention. *For fuck sake,* there is going to be highs and there are going to be lows. *For fuck sake,* your sanity will be pushed to such a limit that you won't be sure if you're going crazy, so you crawl up in a ball and sob, or simply lose your mind. *For fuck sake,* there's going be a lot of sleepless nights. *For fuck sake,* there's going be a lot of worry. *For fuck sake,* this list can go on forever and ever with an entire book dedicated *for fuck sake.* With all of that, there will be tremendous love, tremendous challenges, and tremendous stories to share and memories to hold on to forever. I wish there was a device where all the snapshots of life that you want to remember, you can continuously replay in your head in real time. Wouldn't it be neat to be able to remember all the little details that you swore you would never forget, but somehow became fuzzy over the years? I don't always remember all of the details of all the stories that I promised I would, but I remember the feeling. The feeling of happiness, joy, and peace. I can't quite describe all the moments to someone, but I certainly play it back in my own mind and relive the moments of the smallest little incident that became so special that I can't seem to forget.

I remember one time we took a family vacation with our children. At the time, Matthew was an infant and we drove down to Cape May, New Jersey. I remember sitting on the beach. I have a photo of me with my four children. I remember that specific moment when the picture was taken and the pride I felt for having created those small people. When onlookers would ask if they were all my children, it was such a sense of pride to answer a definite yes. There are a lot of those moments, and although I can't quite articulate how they make me feel, I know how I felt at the time. On the days that I am most overwhelmed with raising children, trying to be my own person, and trying to navigate life, I think back on the simple moments of sitting on the beach posing for a photo with my four small children. I think about how the simplest moment captured a place in my heart. I value all those little moments and how in the grand scheme of life it seems insignificant, but actually makes up a lifetime of beauty. For all my failures and shortcomings, I know one thing I've done right. I've loved completely, I was present, I was committed, I was funny, I was devoted, and mostly, I did the best that I knew how with grace, humility, and an abundance of love.

One last thing. I want to inform you that they may just be listening. I was out with Emma, and was talking about the process of writing this book, and she casually mentioned, "Mom, why don't you include all of the inspirational talks you always give us?" I'll be honest, I was a little taken aback by her comments. She has been listening. All of the car ride talks, the kitchen table chats, the little notes I leave on the door and on the table, they hear and they read. They never let on that they are listening, but they hear what I am saying. Sometimes I think it's in vain, but I've come to realize that they are watching, and they are listening, and they are hearing all that I do. Is it enough? There are plenty of people who do everything that I do, and don't get the results that they envision. I don't know the answer, I may not know the answer for years to come, if ever. What I do know, is that every day I show up. I do my job as their mother to the best of my ability with the purest of heart and the best of intentions. I want to fill their hearts and spirits with hope, the way they have filled mine.

Having children has taught me so many tremendous lessons. I may have taught my own children so many valuable lessons along the way, but at the same time they have taught me as well. Never before have I felt love, devotion, and connection with anyone the way I feel with my children. They are the light in my heart, the pride in my eye, the happiness in my soul. They give me hope, they give me purpose, they give me strength and they give me love. Being a mother is a profoundly generous gift, one that I do not take lightly. I am filled with gratitude that I have this opportunity, and this amazing journey to walk alongside them.